M3 IMAC 2023 USER GUIDE

A Simplified Manual With Complete Step By Step Instructions For Beginners & Seniors On How To Operate The M3 Chip iMac With Tips & Tricks

BY

TERRY HARLEY

Table of Contents

INTRODUCTION

In October 2023, Apple released the 24" M3 iMac, an update to the slim & compact desktop machine released in 2021. The iMac now has an Apple-made M3 chip that replaces the M1 chip, bringing more speed and improving efficiency.

IMAC

FaceTime HD camera | Microphones

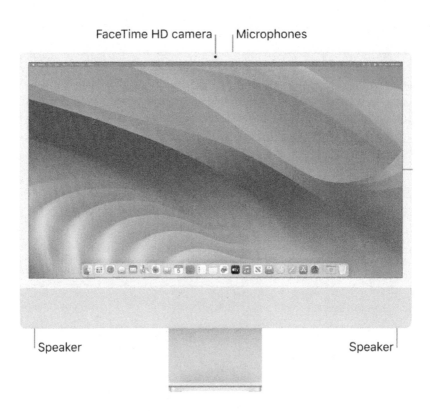

Speaker   Speaker

24-inch iMac with four ports

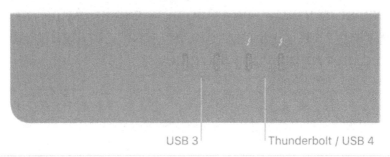

USB 3   Thunderbolt / USB 4

Power connector —   Power button

— 3.5 mm
headphone
jack

FEATURES OF IMAC

Design update

Apple didn't make any design updates to the M3 iMac. The device still has the same slim & compact design as the previous generation iMac. The M3 iMac is available in 7 different colours, which include silver, blue, purple, pink, orange, yellow, & green.

Screen

The M3 chip iMac has a 24" 4.5K Retina screen with 11.30 million pixels, 500 nits brightness, a wide P3 colour gamut, and over a billion colours.

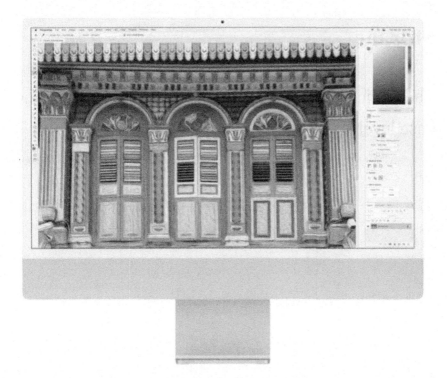

The screen features True Tone technology that automatically changes the screen's colour temperature as the environment changes for a more natural viewing experience.

RAM

The M3 iMac comes with 8GB of integrated memory but can be configured with up to 24GB of memory.

Storage

The device has a storage capacity of up to 2TB. The base level storage begins at 256G.

CHAPTER 1

HOW TO SETUP YOUR MAC

When setting up your iMac, you can personalize some settings, setup features like Touch ID & Siri, and transfer data from another Mac or PC.

When you switch on your iMac for the first time, the Set up Assistant would walk you through the steps you need to get started with your new iMac. You can answer all the prompts, or you can skip a few steps and choose to finish later.

The Setup Assistant will guide you through the following:

→ At the beginning of your iMac setup, you can connect your keyboard, trackpad, & mouse to your Mac
Simply check Chapter 2 of this book to learn more info about connecting a keyboard, trackpad & mouse to your Mac.
→ Choose your language
→ Choose your region or country: This determines the time zone & language of your iMac.

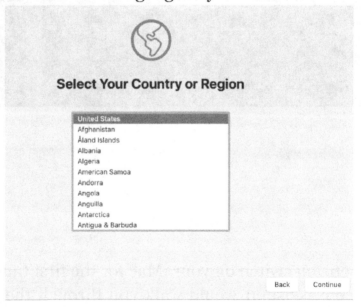

➜ Activate Accessibility features: Check out the accessibility options for Cognitive abilities, Motor, Hearing, & Vision, or click on the **Not Now** option.

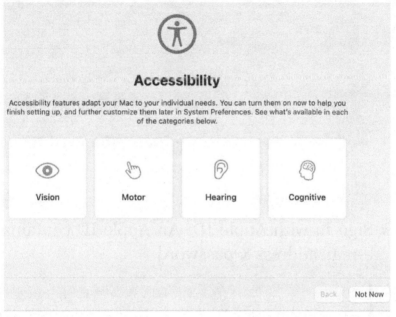

➜ Connect to a WiFi network: Pick one of the WiFi networks, and insert the passcode, if needed. (If you are making use of Ethernet, you can click on the **Other Network Options** button and adhere to the guidelines on the screen).

➜ Migration Information: If you don't want to transfer data from another computer to your iMac, click on the **Not Now** option in the Migration Assistant window.

Migration Assistant

If you have information on another Mac or a Windows PC, you can transfer it to this Mac. You can also transfer information from a Time Machine backup or another startup disk.

How do you want to transfer your information?

From a Mac, Time Machine backup or Startup disk

⦿ From a Windows PC

Not Now   Back   Continue

➔ Sign in with Apple ID: An Apple ID contains an e-mail address & password.

Sign In with Your Apple ID

Sign in to use iCloud, iTunes, App Store, iMessage, FaceTime and more.

Set Up Later

Apple ID [Email]

Create new Apple ID...   Forgot Apple ID or password?

This Mac will be associated with your Apple ID, and data such as photos, contacts and documents will be stored in iCloud so you can access them on other devices. See how your data is managed...

Use different Apple IDs for iTunes and iCloud?

An Apple ID is an account you use for everything you do with Apple —which includes making use of iCloud, Apple Books, Apple TV application, Application Store, Messages, etc. If you do not have an Apple ID, you can create one while setting up your iMac.

➔ Create a computer account: Type your name, account name, & password in the appropriate fields; this information can later be used to unlock your device or confirm certain actions. To change your account login photo, click it, and then pick one of the options.

Create a Computer Account

Fill out the following information to create your computer account.

Full name: Ashley Rico

Account name: ashleyrico

This will be the name of your home folder.

Password: new password   verify

Hint: optional

☑ Allow my Apple ID to reset this password

Back   Continue

→ Save files in iCloud: With the iCloud feature, you can store your files in the cloud, and access them wherever you are. Simply log in with one Apple ID on all your Apple devices.

→ Activate Location Services. Choose whether to let applications like Map use your iMac's location. To change the settings later, click on the Apple menu icon in the menu bar, and then click on Systems Setting in the menu, click on the **Privacy and Security** button in the side bar, and then click on Location Services & select your preferences.

→ Choose whether to share Analytics with Apple & Developers. To change these settings later, click on the Apple menu icon in the menu bar, click on System Settings in the menu, click on the **Privacy and Security** button in the side bar, click Analytics and Improvement, & select your preferences.

→ Setup screen time. This feature helps you to keep track of and get reports on your computer usage. To activate the feature, Click on the **Continue** button, or click on the **Setup Later** button. To setup this feature later, click on the Apple menu icon , click on System Settings, and click on the

Screen Time button in the side bar to select your preferences.

→ Use FileVault to secure your data: FileVault helps protect your data.

→ Activate Siri & Hey Siri: You can enable Siri and "Hey Siri". To setup Siri, click on the **Enable Ask Siri** button. To activate the "Hey Siri" feature, simply say a few Siri commands when asked to.

→ Activate Touch ID: You can add a fingerprint to Touch ID, which you can use to unlock your iMac, authenticate purchases from Apple Books, Apps Store, & iTunes Store, and you can use it to make online purchases with Apple Pay. You can also use Touch ID to login to 3rd-party applications.

→ Setup Apple Pay: Adhere to the guidelines on your screen to configure Apple Pay

→ Choose your look: Choose Auto, Dark, or Light for your desktop look. If you want to change what you choose, click on the Apple menu icon in the upper left corner of your display, click on System Settings in the menu, click on Appearance, and then pick one of the options.

CHAPTER 2

MOUSE, TRACKPAD, & KEYBOARD

Connect accessories to your iMac

You can connect your Mac to other devices, such as a trackpad, mouse, or keyboard; wearable devices such as AirPods; & others.

Get Started. Before connecting the device to your iMac, do the following:

- Go through the documentation that came with the accessory.
- Ensure your Mac is running the latest version of macOS

Connect the wireless device

Activate Bluetooth. Click on the Control Centre icon⚏ in the menu bar at the upper part of your display. The Bluetooth icon❁ is blue when enabled. If the Bluetooth icon is gray, click the icon to activate Bluetooth.

Pair a Bluetooth device. The 1st time you use a Bluetooth device on your Mac, you need to pair it. Check the manual that came with the Bluetooth device to ensure it's ready to pair— for example, you might have to press a button to activate Bluetooth on the device. Your iMac & the Bluetooth device must be switched on and close to each other.

When the Bluetooth device is ready to pair, Select Apple menu in the top left corner of your display, click on System Setting in the menu that pops up, and click on the **Bluetooth** button in the sidebar. Choose the Bluetooth device in the Nearby Device list, and then click on the **Connect** button.

Connect a Bluetooth device. Your Bluetooth device will automatically connect to your iMac after you have paired it. To see which Bluetooth devices you've connected to your iMac, click the Control Center icon in the menu bar at the upper right part of your display, then move the cursor over Bluetooth and click on the arrow.

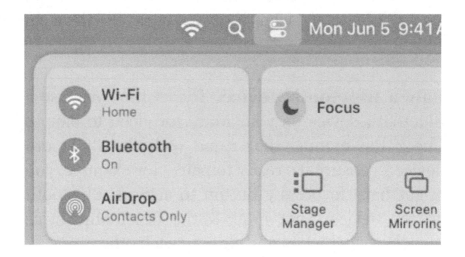

The accessories that have a blue icon in the list are connected to your iMac.

If an accessory is not automatically connecting, select Apple menu in the top left corner of your display, click on System Setting in the menu that pops-up, and click on **Bluetooth** on the side bar. Ensure the Bluetooth accessory is in the **My Device** list. If you can't find it there, adhere to the directives above to pair the device.

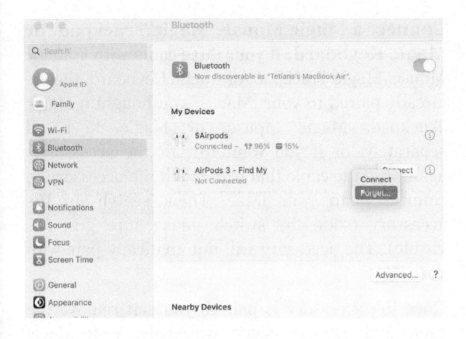

Disconnect or forget a Bluetooth device. To disconnect a Bluetooth device, select Apple menu in the top left corner of your display, click on System Setting in the menu that pops-up, and then click on Bluetooth in the Sidebar. Hover the cursor over the Bluetooth accessory in the **My Device** list, and click on the **Disconnect** button when it appears. To forget a Bluetooth device so your iMac does not connect automatically, click the Info icon beside the Bluetooth device, then click the **Forget Device** button.

Connect a Magic Mouse, Magic Trackpad, or Magic Keyboard. If your iMac came with a Magic Mouse, Magic Trackpad, or Magic Keyboard, they're already paired to your iMac. If you bought a Magic Trackpad, Magic Mouse, or Magic Keyboard separately, or if you want to pair the accessories again, use the cable that came with the accessory to connect it to your iMac. Then, switch on the accessory (slide the switch, make sure green is visible). The accessory will automatically pair with your iMac

Once the accessory is paired, you can remove the cable and use the device wirelessly. Your Magic Mouse, Magic Trackpad, or Magic Keyboard will automatically connect to your iMac when Bluetooth is enabled.

Magic Mouse

Here are some general tips for using the Magic Mouse.

Switch off/on: Slide the off/on switch on the mouse to switch it on (green means On).

Click: Use a finger to press the upper surface of the mouse.

Secondary click (i.e., right-click): use your finger to press the right or left part of your mouse. Or press the Ctrl button on the keyboard while clicking the mouse.

360° scroll: Pan or scroll in the direction you want by brushing along the mouse surface with a finger.

Zoom: Press & hold the Control button, and scroll with a finger to zoom in on things on your display.

To activate display zoom, select Apple menu , click on Systems Setting, click on the **Accessibility** button, click on Zoom then choose **Use Scroll Gesture with Modifier Key to Zoom**

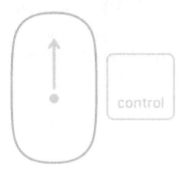

Swipe with two fingers: Swipe to the right or left to surf through pictures, pages, etc.

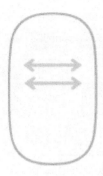

Change the mouse settings. To change mouse settings like scroll speed, tracking, and more, simply click on the **Mouse** button in Systems Settings.

Magic keyboard

The wireless keyboard that comes with your iMac has inbuilt features that perform many system functions with the touch of a button, including adding emoji, changing the keyboard language, locking your Mac, and many others. The Touch ID Magic Keyboard allows you to use a registered fingerprint to log in & make purchases with Apple Pay.

Function keys (F1 to F12)

On/off switch

Touch ID

Function (Fn)/Globe key

Switch the keyboard off or on. Slide the off/on switch on the keyboard to switch it on or off (green is on). If your Mac does not recognize the keyboard, simply use a USB-C to Lightning Cable to connect it to your Mac to pair it, and then remove the cable. Charge the keyboard with the same USB-C to Lightning Cable.

Lock your iMac. Press Touch ID or the Lock button. To unlock your iMac, touch the **Touch ID** sensor or press one of the keys on the keyboard and type your passcode.

Configure Touch ID. You can use your registered fingerprint to unlock your iMac and make purchases in many applications & sites using Apple Pay. If you didn't setup Touch ID when setting up your iMac, you can set it up later in the Touch ID and Passcode settings in System Settings.

Use Touch ID. Gently put your registered finger on the Touch ID sensor. When you first turn on or restart your iMac, you must enter your password to log in to your iMac. After that, you can use Touch ID whenever you are asked for a passcode.

Configure keyboard options: To set options for the keyboard and Function (Fn)/Globe key⊕ , select Apple menu, click on Systems Setting, click on Keyboard, and select options for changing the keyboard or input source, displaying emoji and symbols, starting dictation, or defining functions.

Use emoji or change keyboard language: Press the Globe button⊕ to move to another keyboard. Press the Globe key⊕ several times to move to the other language or emoji options you choose in the Keyboard settings.

Use the function keys. The function keys provide shortcuts to the following system functions:

→ Brightness (F1, F2): Press the brightness down key ☼ or the brightness key ☼ to decrease or increase the screen brightness

→ Mission Control (F3): Press the Mission Control key ⊟ to see what is running on your device, including all spaces and open windows.

→ Spotlight Search (F4): Press the Spotlight button ⌕ to launch Spotlight and search for items on your device.

→ Siri/Dictation (F5): Press the Microphone button 🎤 to turn on dictation—you can dictate text in any application that allows text editing. Hold down the Microphone button 🎤 to activate Siri, and then say your request.

→ DND (F6): Press the DND button ☾ to enable or disable Do Not Disturb. When DND is active, you will not hear or see notifications on your device, but you can check the Notification Centre to see if you have any notifications.

→ Media (F7, F8, F9): Press the Rewind key ◁◁ to rewind, the Play/Pause key ▷|| to pause or play, or the Fast Forward key ▷▷ to fast-forward songs, movies, or slideshows.

→ Silent (F10): Press the Mute key ◁ to mute the sound from the internal speakers.

→ Volume (F11, F12): Press the volume down key ◁ʼ or the volume up key ◁⁾⁾⁾ to increase or reduce the volume of your device.

Keyboard shortcuts

To get things done faster on your iMac, you can use combinations called keyboard shortcuts. A keyboard shortcut consists of a modifier key(s) (like Command or Control) and another key, pressed simultaneously. For example, hold down the Command key and then press the C key on your keyboard to copy an item

View keyboard shortcuts

Shortcuts appear beside menu items in macOS applications.

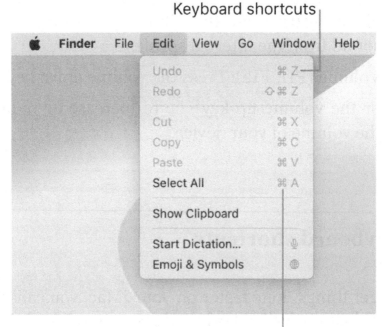

Keyboard shortcuts

Symbols represent modifier keys.

Personalize keyboard shortcuts

You can create some keyboard shortcuts by changing key combinations.

→ Click on the Apple menu icon, click on System Setting, click on Keyboard on the side bar, and click on Keyboard Shortcuts on the right part of the window.

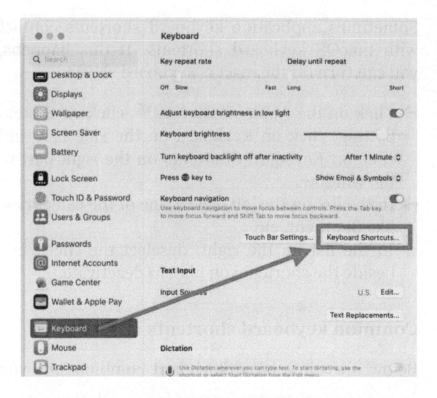

→ In the list on the left, select one of the categories, like Spotlight, etc.
→ In the list on the right, select the check box beside the shortcut you plan on changing.
→ Double-click the current combination, then press another combination.
→ To use the new keyboard shortcuts, quit & reopen the application you want to use the shortcut for.

Disable a keyboard shortcut

Sometimes application keyboard shortcuts conflict with macOS keyboard shortcuts. If this happens, you can turn off the macOS keyboard shortcut.

➔ Click on the Apple menu icon, click on System Setting, click on Keyboard on the side bar, and click on Keyboard Shortcuts on the right part of the window.
➔ In the list on the left, select one of the categories, like Spotlight, etc.
➔ In the list on the right, deselect the check box beside the shortcut you plan to deactivate.

Common keyboard shortcuts

Below are some basic keyboard combinations you can use to perform basic tasks on your device.

➔ Cmd-X: Cut the highlighted items and copy them.
➔ Cmd-C: Copy the highlighted items.
➔ Cmd-V: Paste the copied items in the new document or application.
➔ Command-Z: Undo the last command. Press the Cmd-Shift-Z to redo the command.
➔ Cmd-A: Highlight all the items.

→ Command-F: launch the search window or look for things in a doc.

→ Cmd-H: Conceal the front application window. Press the Cmd-Option-H combination to see the front application but conceal every other application

→ Cmd-M: Minimize the front window

→ Command-N: Launch a new window or doc.

→ Cmd-O: Open the highlighted items, or launch a dialog to highlight a file to open.

→ Cmd-P: Print the document.

→ Cmd-S: Save the file.

→ Command-Q: close the present application

→ Cmd-Option-Esc: Select an application to Force Quit.

Magic Trackpad

You can do a lot on your iMac with basic trackpad gestures.

Click: press anywhere on your iMac's track-pad. Or activate the "Tap to click" feature in Trackpad Settings, so that you can perform the **Click** feature by simply tapping.

Force click: Click & press deeper. With the Force-Click feature, you can find more information about something, for instance, click on a word to check out its meaning.

Zoom: Put 2 of your fingers on the trackpad and pinch open or closed to zoom in or out of web pages & images.

Open Launchpad: Pinch closed with 4 or 5 fingers, then click on an application to launch it.

Swipe between applications: To move from one full-screen application to another, just swipe right or left with 3 or 4 of your fingers.

Two-finger scroll: Slide down or up with 2 of your fingers to scroll

Secondary/right-click: Click with 2 fingers. Or press the Control button on your keyboard & click the trackpad

Swipe to navigate: Use 2 of your fingers to swipe to the right or left to flip through docs, web pages, etc.

Personalize your gestures. Select Apple menu 🍎, click on Systems Setting, then click on Trackpad in the side bar. You can carry out the following:

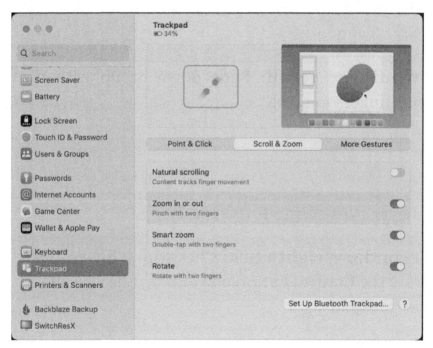

➜ Get more info about gestures

→ Adjust the click pressure to the pressure you want to use
→ Personalize other track-pad features

Watch a video

→ To see your Mac's trackpad gestures & a short video showing every gesture, select the Apple menu , click on Systems Settings, and then click on the Trackpad button on the sidebar. (You may need to scroll down.)
→ To see your Mac's mouse gestures & a short video showing every gesture, select the Apple menu , click on Systems Settings, and then click on the Mouse button on the sidebar. (You may need to scroll down.)
You can also disable or personalize gestures in the Mouse settings.

Charge the batteries in your accessories

The Magic Trackpad, Magic Mouse, & Magic Keyboard all have internal rechargeable batteries.

To check the battery level, click the Control Centre icon 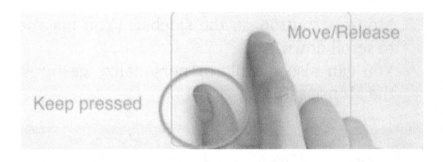 in the menu bar, click on the Bluetooth icon ⃰, and select the device.

To charge the battery, just use a USB-C to Lightning Cable to connect the accessory to your iMac.

Drag & drop an item

You can drag and drop items on your iMac.

→ On your iMac, select the item you want to drag, like a picture or text.
→ Hold down the trackpad or mouse while dragging the object to another location.

Move/Release

Keep pressed

To copy the item instead of moving it, hold down the Option key on the keyboard while dragging.
→ Release the mouse or trackpad to drop the item in another location.

CHAPTER 3

FIND YOUR WAY AROUND YOUR IMAC

The Desktop

The desktop is the first thing you see on the iMac. The menu bar is located at the upper part of your iMac's desktop and the dock can be found at the lower part of the desktop.

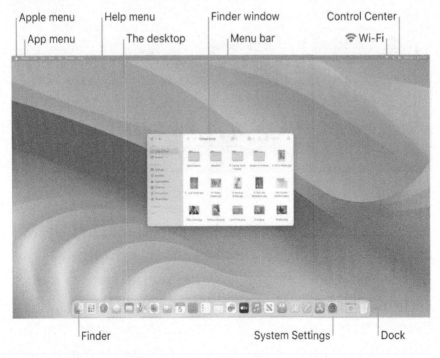

Tip: Can't see the cursor on your display? To make it bigger temporarily, slide the mouse back & forth quickly.

The desktop is where you open & use applications, work on files, search your device or the internet using Spotlight, etc. To change your desktop wallpaper, launch Systems Settings, click on the **Wallpaper** button, and choose one of the options.

Menu bar: The menus bar can be found at the upper part of your display. You can utilize the menus on the left part of the menu bar to select commands & perform tasks in applications. The items on the menu bar change, depending on the app you are making use of. You can use the icons on the right part of the menu bar to check your WiFi status 📶 , connect to a WiFi network, open the Control Centre 🎛, search with Spotlight 🔍 , view your battery usage 🔋 , etc.

Apple menu: The Apple menu contains items you use very often and can be found in the top left edge of your display. Click on the Apple icon to launch it.

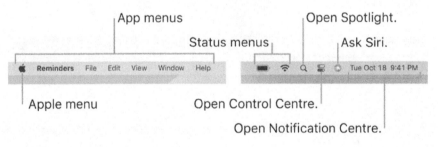

Application menu: You can have more than one window & app open at the same time. The name of the active app will be displayed in bold on the right side of the Apple menu , as well as the unique menus of that app. If you launch another application or click on an open window in another application, the name of the application menu will change to that app, & the menus in the menu bar will also change.

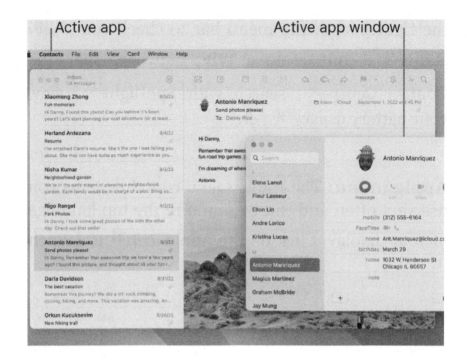

Finder on iMac

The Finder, represented by a blue smiley face icon 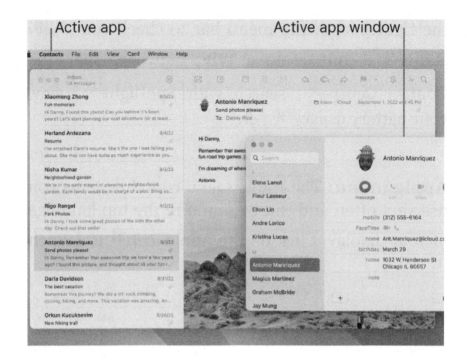, is the home base of your iMac. You use the Finder to organize & gain access to almost everything on your iMac, including videos, pictures, documents, and other files. Click on the Finder icon in the Dock at the lower part of your display to open a Finder window.

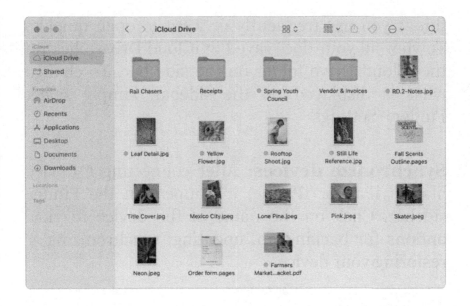

Stay organized. Your iMac has folders designed for common types of content—Music, Apps, Pictures, Documents, Downloads, etc. As you create documents, install applications, and perform other tasks, you can create new folders to remain organized. To create a new folder, select File in the upper part of your display, and then click on the **New Folder** button in the menu that appears.

The Finder window: To change how folders & documents are displayed, click on the pop-up menu icon at the upper part of the Finder window. You can view them in a gallery⬚, in hierarchical columns⬚, in a list view⬚, or as icons⬚. The side bar on the left side of the window displays the things you use frequently or want to open quickly. To view all your docs saved in iCloud Drive, click on the iCloud Drive folder on the side bar. To change what is displayed on the sidebar, simply select Finder> Settings

Synchronize devices: After connecting a device like an iPad or iPhone, it'll appear in the Finder sidebar. Click on the name of the device to view options for backing up, updating, synchronizing & restoring your device.

Gallery view: Gallery View and Column view allow you to see a big overview of your selected files so that you can easily identify your videos, pictures, & other documents. The Preview panel on the right displays info that can help you identify the file you're looking for. Use the scrubber bar in the lower part of the window to quickly find what you are looking for. Press Shift-Command-P to open or close the preview panel. To display the Preview panel options in the Finder, select View> Show Preview. To customize what is displayed, select View> Show Preview Options, then select options for the type of file.

Tip: To show file names in Gallery view, press Command-J & choose Show file name.

Quick Actions:

In Column or Gallery view, click on the More Options icon ⊙ in the lower right corner of the Finder window to see shortcuts that you can use to manage & edit files in the Finder.

Combine PDFs, trim audio and video files, and automate tasks.

The Dock

The Dock, in the lower part of your desktop, is a convenient place to store documents & applications you use very often.

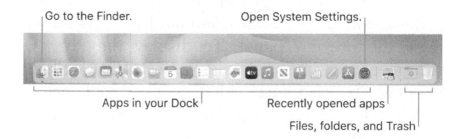

Go to the Finder.   Open System Settings.

Apps in your Dock   Recently opened apps
                         Files, folders, and Trash

Open an item in the Dock

Carry out any of the below in the Dock on your iMac:

→ Launch an application: Click on the app's icon. For instance, click on the Finder icon to open a Finder window.

→ Open a file in an application by dragging the file to the application's icon. For instance, you can open a document you created in the Pages application, by dragging the document over the Pages application icon in the Dock.

→ Display an item in the Finder: Cmd-click the icon of the item.

➔ Go to the previous application & hide the application you are currently using: Option-click the icon of the application you are currently using.
➔ Switch to another application & hide every other app: Option-Cmd-click the icon of the application you want to use.

Close an application: Click on the red dot in the upper left part of an open window to close the window (the app will remain open). Open applications have black dots under them on the Dock. To close an application, ctrl-click on the app's icon in the Dock then click the **Quit** button.

Indicates an open app

Remove or add Dock items

Carry out any of the below on your device:

➜ Add an application, file, or folder to the Dock: You can add an app to the Dock by simply dragging the app to the left side of the Dock. Drag folders & files to the right side of the Dock.

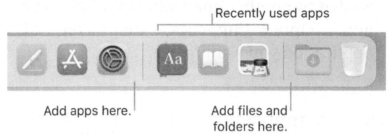

Recently used apps

Add apps here. Add files and folders here.

➜ Remove items from the Dock: You can remove an item from the Dock by simply dragging it out of the Dock.

Personalize the Dock

➜ On your iMac, click Apple menu, click on Systems Settings, and then click on Desktop & Dock in the side bar.

➜ Under Dock on the right side of the window, make changes to any of the options.

For example, you can change the size of the icons in the Dock, the location of the Dock, or even hide the Dock.

Click on the Help button ? in the lower part of the window to get more info about the options.

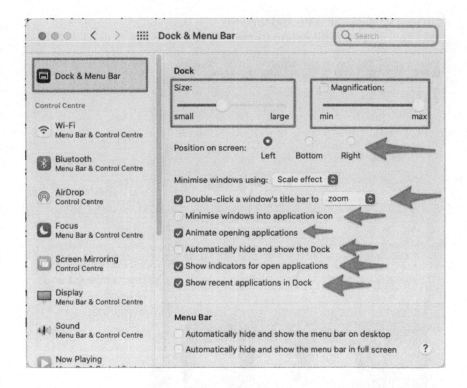

Notifications Center

In the Notifications Center, you can keep up with notifications you've missed and use widgets to check the top headlines, the weather, etc.

Click the date and time to
open Notification Center.

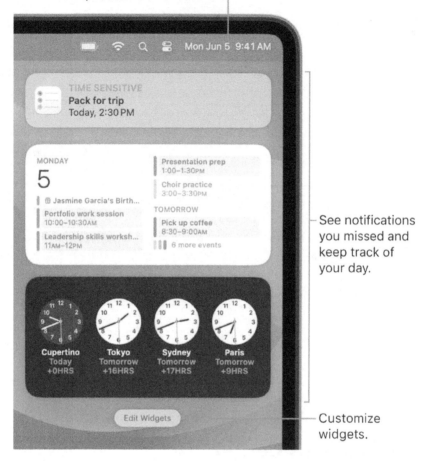

See notifications
you missed and
keep track of
your day.

Customize
widgets.

Open or close the Notifications Center

→ To open the Notification Centre, simply click on
the time & date in the menu bar, or use 2 fingers
to swipe to the left from the right edge of your
iMac's trackpad.

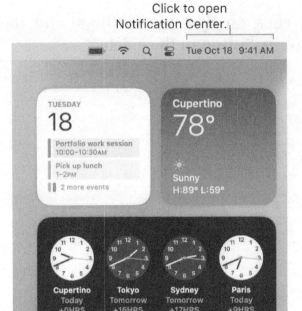

Click to open
Notification Center.

→ To close the Notifications Centre, simply click anywhere on your desktop or click on the time & date in the menu bar.

Focus: When you are at work, eating dinner, or just don't want to be disturbed, the Focus feature can automatically filter your alerts so you only see specific ones. Focus can block all notifications or allow only some to appear, and it can use statuses in the Messages application to let your contacts know that your notifications have been silenced. To configure the Focus feature, click on the Apple menu icon, click on Systems Settings, and then click on the **Focus** button in the sidebar.

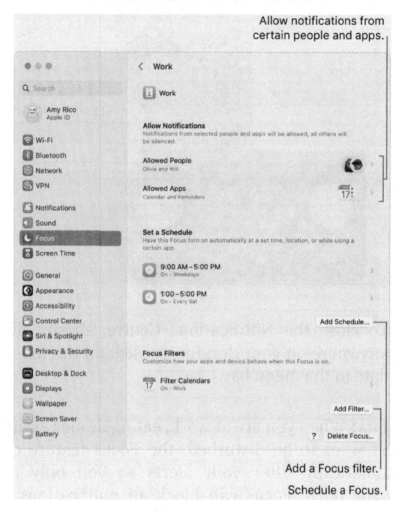

You can personalize the Focus feature to suit what you are doing at the moment and only receive notifications from certain individuals or applications.

To enable or disable the Focus feature, click on the Controls Center icon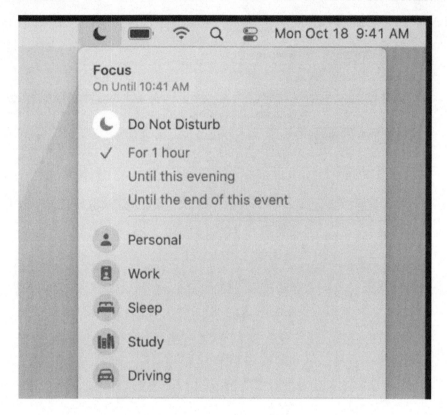 in the menu bar, and then click on the Focus segment & pick one of the Focus modes.

Interact with your alerts: Reply to emails, listen to podcasts, or check calendar event details. Click on the arrow in the upper right edge of a notification to see options, take actions, or get more info.

Configure notification settings: Click on the Apple menu icon 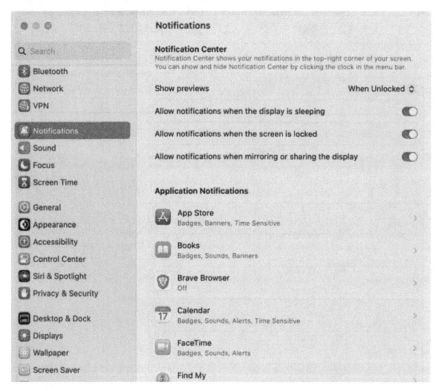, click on Systems Settings, click on the **Notifications** button, and then choose which notifications you'd like to see.

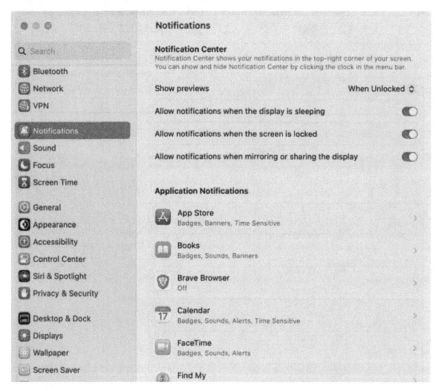

Customize your widgets: Click the Edit Widgets button to remove, add, or re-organize widgets.

Control Center

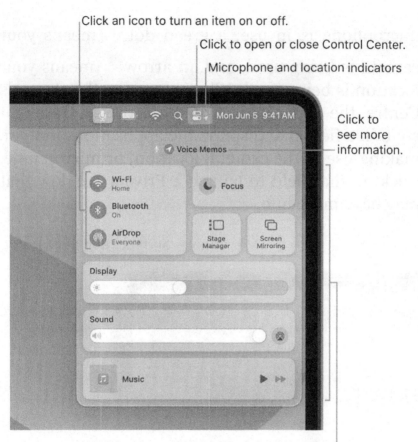

Click an icon to turn an item on or off.

Click to open or close Control Center.

Microphone and location indicators

Click to see more information.

For some controls, click to see more options.
For Stage Manger, click to turn it on or off.

The Controls Center provides quick access to important macOS settings like Focus, WiFi, or AirDrop . You can personalize the Control Centre to add other features, like battery status, accessibility shortcuts, etc.

When you see an orange dot beside the Control Centre icon in the menu bar, it means your iMac's microphone is in use; a green dot ⬤ means your camera is being used, and an arrow ➤ means your location is being used. When you open the Controls Centre, the upper part of the Controls Centre might contain a field that displays the applications that are making use of the camera, location, or microphone. Click on that field to launch a Privacy window that may have more info.

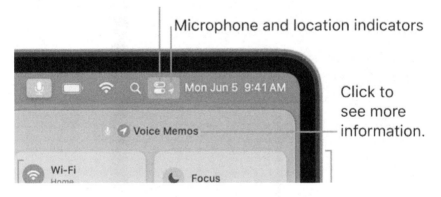

Microphone and location indicators

Click to see more information.

Use the Controls Center

➔ Click on the Controls Center icon 🎚 in the menus bar.
➔ Carry out any of the below with items in the Controls Center:
  • Move a slider to reduce or increase a setting.
  • Click on an icon to enable or disable a feature, for instance, click Bluetooth or AirDrop to enable or disable it

- Click an item or the item's arrow to display more options— for instance, click on the **Focus** button to display your Focus list and activate or disable a Focus mode.

Personalize the Controls Center

→ Click the Apple menu icon, click on Systems Settings, and then click on Control Centre on the sidebar.

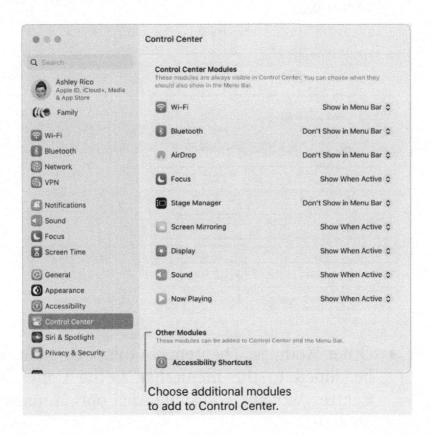

Choose additional modules to add to Control Center.

→ Select the settings for the items in these segments on the right side of the window.

- Controls Centre Modules: The components of this segment are always displayed in the Controls Centre; you cannot remove these items from the Controls Centre. You can choose to display these items in the menus bar. Click on the drop-down menu beside an item, and then pick any of the options.

- Menu bar only: You can add more items to the menu bar.

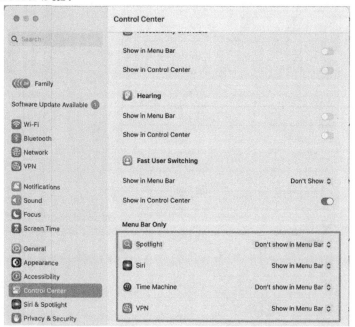

- Other Modules: The items in this segment can be added to the menu bar & the Controls Centre. Activate or disable each option under an item.

Launchpad

Launchpad is a central location on your iMac where you can browse & launch applications. After installing an application from the App Store, it will appear in Launchpad.

Click to open an app.

Drag an app over another to create a folder.

Click the dots or swipe to see more apps.

Open & close Launchpad

→ Click on the Launchpad icon in the Dock to enter Launchpad

Launchpad arranges your apps in a grid.
Click an app icon to open it.

Folder containing apps

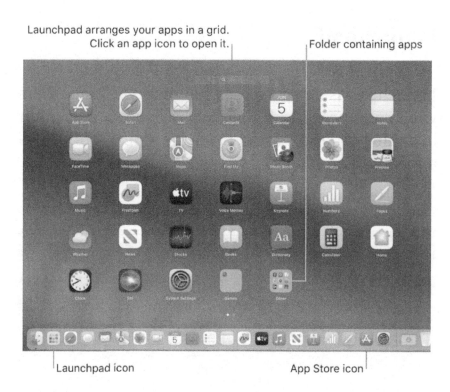

Launchpad icon   App Store icon

→ Press the Esc key to close Launchpad without launching an app.

Find & launch applications in Launchpad

→ Find an application: Type the app's name in the search box in the upper part of Launchpad. Or, check the next page in Launchpad—Press Cmd-Right Arrow or Command-Left Arrow, or use one of your fingers to swipe right or left on your trackpad.

→ Click on an application's icon to open it

Organize applications in Launchpad

→ You can move an application on a page by dragging the application to another location on the same page.

→ You can move an application to another page by dragging the application to the edge of your iMac screen, and then releasing the application when you enter the next page.

→ You can create an application folder by dragging an application over another application.

→ Change the name of a folder: Click on the folder to open it, click on the folder's name, and then type a name.

→ To add more apps to the folder, simply drag the apps over the folder.

→ You can remove an application from a folder by dragging the application out of the folder.

Remove applications from Launchpad

→ In Launchpad, long-click an application till all the applications start jiggling.

→ Click on the application's Delete icon⊗

System Settings

You can personalize all your iMac's settings in Systems Setting. For instance, you can change your desktop wallpaper in Wallpaper settings. You can also download new software updates.

Personalize your device.

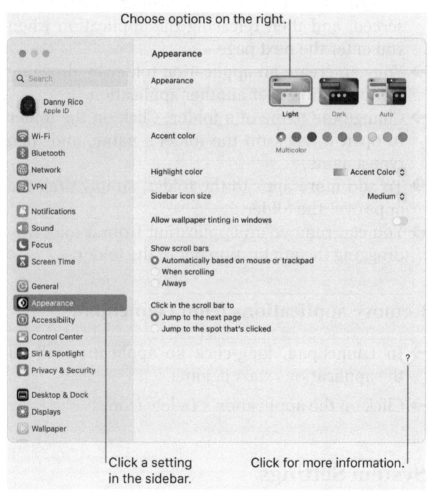

Choose options on the right.

Click a setting in the sidebar.

Click for more information.

Click on the Systems Settings icon 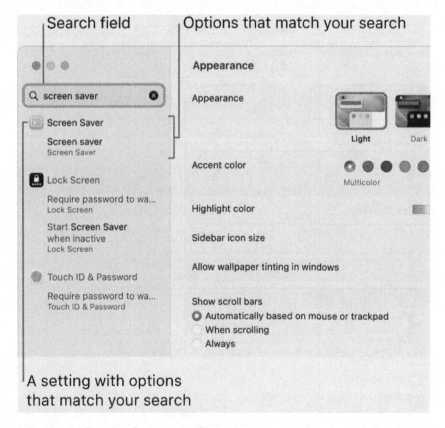 on the Dock or click on the Apple menu icon, click on Systems Setting, and then click on any of the settings in the sidebar that you'd like to customize. You may need to scroll down to see additional settings.

Find options in the System Settings

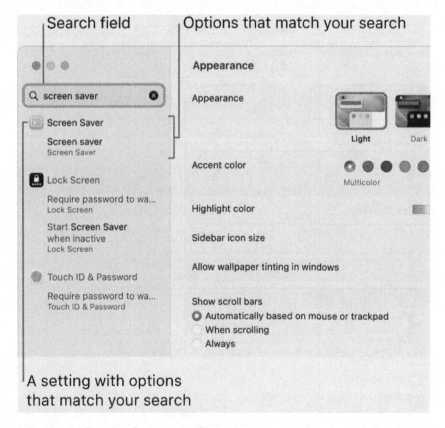

Search field

Options that match your search

A setting with options that match your search

If you don't know where a certain setting is in System Setting, use the search box in the upper left part of the window. Settings with options that match what you typed will be displayed below.

Update macOS: Click the Apple menu icon, click on System Setting, click the **General** button, and then click Software Updates to see if your iMac is using the latest version of macOS software. You can set the automatic software update option.

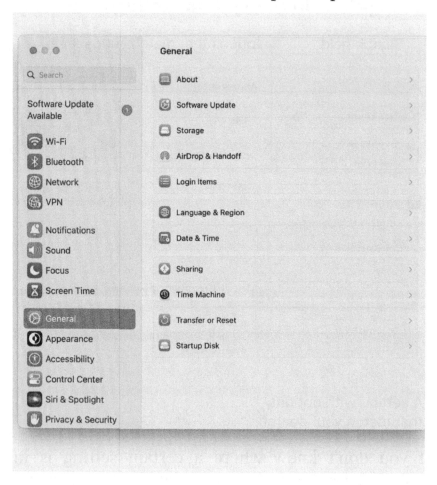

Spotlight

With the Spotlight feature, you can easily find anything on your device, like contacts, files, pictures, e-mails, etc. You can also use Spotlight to launch applications or perform quick actions, like setting an alarm or running a shortcut.

Start typing, and results appear quickly.

Find something

➔ Carry out any of the below:

➢ Click on the Spotlight icon Q in the menus bar at the upper part of your display.

➢ Press Command-Space bar to display or hide the Spotlight search box.

➢ Press the Spotlight key Q in the Fn keys row

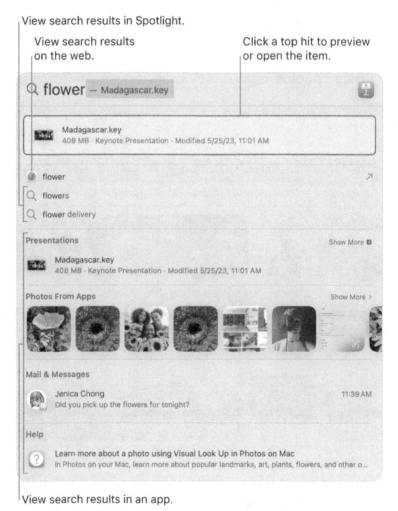

View search results in Spotlight.

View search results on the web.

Click a top hit to preview or open the item.

View search results in an app.

→ Type what you want in the search bar.

→ Click one of the results in the search results.

→ To view all the results from your iMac in the Finder, scroll to the end of the results list, then click the **Search in Finder** button.

Get conversions & calculations in Spotlight

You can enter mathematical expressions, currency rates, temperatures, or measurements in the Spotlight search bar and get conversions or calculations in the search field.

0.012	short tons
400	ounces
11,339.81	grams
11,339,809.25	milligrams

→ For Calculations: Enter a mathematical expression like 355 * 25.68 or 2445/64.

→ To convert currency: Enter an amount for instance $260, 460 krone, or "250 yen in euros".

→ Temperature Conversion: Enter a temperature for example 87.5F, 82C, or 303K in F.

→ Measurement Conversion: Enter measurements for example 30lbs, 55yards, 44stone, or "95ft to meters".

→ World clock conversion: Type a short sentence about the time in a place, like "UK local time" or "time in France."

Apple ID on iMac

Your Apple ID is an account that allows you to gain access to all Apple services. When you have an Apple ID, you can download applications from the Applications Store; gain access to media in Apple TV, Apple Podcasts, Apple Music, & Apple Books; Update content on all your devices using iCloud; setup a family sharing group; etc.

Note: If you forget your Apple ID passcode, you do not have to setup another Apple ID. Simply, click on "Forget Apple ID or Password"? link in the login window to retrieve your passcode.

All in one place: Control everything related to your Apple ID in one place. Enter Systems Settings

—you'll find your Apple ID & Family Sharing settings in the upper part of the side bar. Click on the **Sign in with your Apple ID** button to log in with your Apple ID if you have not done that before.

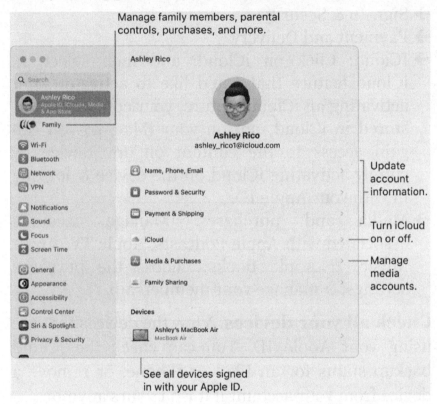

Update your security, account, & payment info. In Systems Setting, click on your Apple ID in the side bar at the upper left corner of the window, then choose one of the items to review & update your account details.

→ Overview: The Overview segment allows you to know if your account is setup & working properly - otherwise you can find tips & information here.

→ Personal Information

→ Sign-In & Security

→ Payment and Delivery

→ ICloud: Click on iCloud, and then select an iCloud feature that you'd like to activate. After activating an iCloud feature, your content will be stored in iCloud, not on your iMac, so you can gain access to the content on any device by simply activating iCloud on the device & logging in with your Apple ID.

→ Media and purchases: Manage accounts associated with Apple Podcasts, Apple TV, Apple Music, & Apple Books; choose the purchase settings; & manage your membership.

Check all your devices. View the devices that are using your Apple ID. You can check the iCloud backup status for an iPad or iPhone, or remove a device from your account if it isn't yours anymore.

Family Sharing

The Family Sharing feature allows you to create a family group (consisting of about 5 members) where you can share & manage purchases, share device locations, etc. You can also control how your child uses their device by creating an Apple ID account for the child and setting Screen Time limits. To manage Family Sharing settings, click on Family in Systems settings, then select the options you want on the right side of the window.

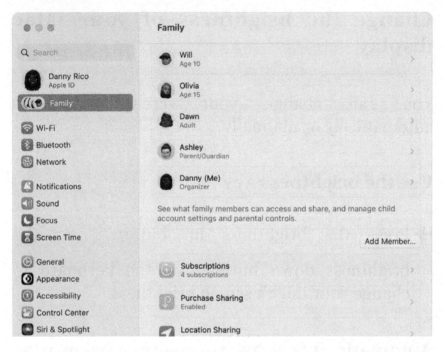

Share storage & purchases with Family Sharing. Members of the Family Sharing group can share purchases from the Apps Store, iTunes Store, Apple Books, & Apple TV application, and also share the same storage plan. You can pay for the group purchases with your card & also approve your child's spending from your device

CHAPTER 4

FUNDAMENTALS

Change the brightness of your iMac display

You can change your screen brightness automatically or manually.

Use the brightness key

→ Press the brightness up button ☼ or the brightness down button ☼ on the keyboard to change your iMac's screen brightness.

Automatically change your screen brightness

Your iMac can use its ambient light sensor to automatically change your screen brightness to match the lighting around you.

→ Click on Apple menu , click Systems Setting, and then click on the Displays button on the sidebar.

→ Enable the **"Automatically adjust brightness"** setting on the right side of the window.

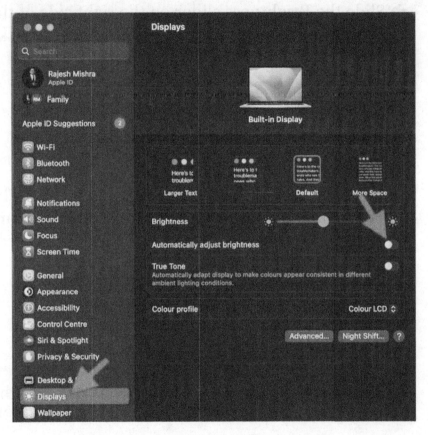

If you can't find the "Automatically adjust brightness" option, you can adjust the brightness manually.

Adjust the brightness manually

➔ Click on Apple menu, click on Systems Setting, and then click on the Displays button in the sidebar.
➔ Slide the Brightness slider on the right side of the window to change your iMac's screen brightness.

Connect your iMac to the Internet

You can connect to the Internet with your Mac. The 2 most common ways to access the Internet are through a WiFi (wireless) or Ethernet (wired) connection.

Use WiFi

If a WiFi network is available, the WiFi button will be displayed in the menu bar. Click on the button, and then pick one of the networks to join. If there's a lock icon next to the name of the network, it means the network is password-protected - you must insert the WiFi passcode before you can make use of the network.

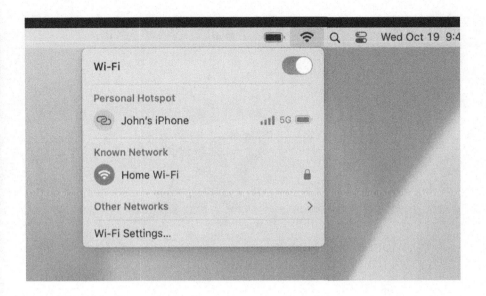

Using Ethernet

Use an Ethernet either through an Ethernet network or via a cable modem or DSL. Use an adapter to connect the Ethernet cable to the Thunderbolt or USB port on your device.

In most cases, your iMac will be connected to the Internet automatically. If not, follow the steps below to access network settings. If you are not sure what to enter, contact your internet service provider or network administrator.

→ Click the Apple menu icon in the upper left corner of your display, and then click on Systems Settings

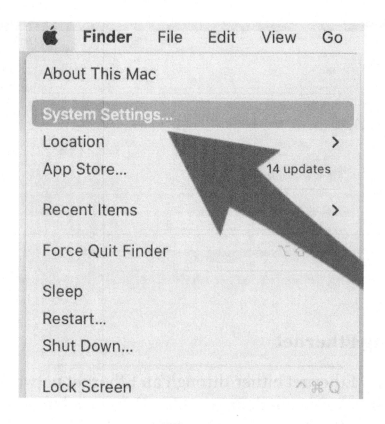

➔ Click on Network in the sidebar, click on the Ethernet Service on the right side of the window, and then click on the **Details** button.

→ Activate or deactivate Limit IP Address Tracking if you wish.

→ Click on TCP / IP on the sidebar, select the Configure IPv4 drop-down menu, and select the configuration method recommended by your ISP (internet service provider).

- Use DHCP: Select this option if you've received an IP address automatically from your internet service provider.

- Use DHCP with manual address: Select this option if you were sent a specific IP address & your internet service provider uses DHCP, select it, and then insert the IP address.

- Manually: Select this option if your internet service provider sent a specific IP address, a router address, & a subnet mask to you, and then insert those values.

→ If you were sent DNS server or search domain settings, click on DNS in the side bar and then insert the details you received.

→ If you were sent WINS settings, click on the WINS button in the side bar and then insert the details you received.

→ If you received Ethernet hardware settings, click on the **Hardware** button in the sidebar, and then insert the info you received

→ If you were sent proxy server settings, click on the Proxy button in the side bar and then insert the details you received.
→ Click **OK**.

View & edit files with Quick Look

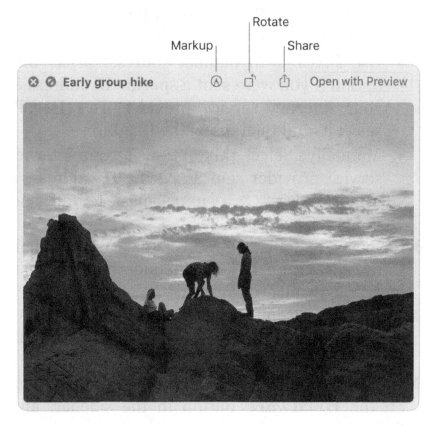

The **Quick Look** feature provides a quick, full-size overview of almost any file without opening it. You can rotate pictures, trim videos & audio, and use Mark-up - in the Quick Look window.

→ Select an item (Hover the cursor over the item, and then click on the item to select it) or select multiple items (Hold down the Command button on your keyboard, and then click the items), and then press the Space bar on your keyboard.

→ Carry out any of the below in the Quick Look window:

- Change the size of the window: Click on the Full-Screen icon ⊘ in the upper left corner of the window or drag the window's corners. To leave full-screen, hover the cursor to the lower part of the window, and then click the Shrink icon ⬎ that appears.

- Click on the Rotate Left icon ⬑ to rotate the item or long-press the Option button on the keyboard, and then click on the Rotate Right icon ⬏. Keep clicking on the icon to continue rotating the item.

- Zoom out & in of an item: Press Cmd-+ to zoom in or Cmd-minus keyboard combination to zoom out.

- Trim audio or video clips: Click on the Trim icon ▸☐◂, and then drag the yellow handle in the trim tab. Click on the Play icon ▶ to preview the adjustments you've made. Click the **Revert** button to start over. When you are ready to save the adjustments you've made, click on the **Done** button then replace the original file or save it as a new file.

- Click on the Markup icon Ⓐ to mark up an item.

- Share an item: click the Share icon ⬆, and then select one of the sharing options.

- Copy the item's subject: If the item is a picture, you can isolate the photo's subject from the background. Ctrl-click the picture, then click on the **Copy Subject** button. You can paste the subject in a note, e-mail, or document.

→ When you are done, press the Space bar or click on the Close icon ❌ to close the Quick View window.

Increase or reduce your Mac's volume

→ Click on the Sound controls icon 🔊 in the Controls Center or menu bar, and then drag the Sound slider to the right or left to increase or reduce the volume level.

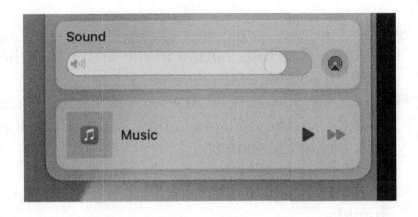

If you do not see the Sounds control icon in the menu bar, you can add it, to do this; simply click on the Apple menu icon in the upper left corner of your display, click on the **Systems Settings** button in the menu, and then click on Controls Center in the sidebar. Click on the drop-down menu beside Sound on the right side of the window, and then pick an option.

→ Use the volume buttons in the FN keys row on your keyboard.

Change your Mac's alert sounds

When you're about to do something that's not allowed, or your iMac needs input or more info, an alert message will appear on the display & an alert sound will play. You can change the sound of the alert & adjust its volume.

→ Click on the Apple menu icon, click on the **System Settings** button in the menu, and then click on Sounds in the sidebar.
→ Click on the drop-down menu beside "Alert sounds" on the right side of the window and then pick any of the sounds.
An alert tone will play when it's selected.
→ Carry out any of the below to adjust the alert sound:
  - Change alert volume level: Move the Alert volume slider.
  - If you want to hear a startup sound when you restart your iMac, activate the **Play sound on startup** feature.
  - Hear user interface sound effects: Your iMac will play sound effects when you carry out certain actions, like when you drag something to the trash. To deactivate these sound effects, disable the "Play users interface sounds effect" feature.
  - Hear sound effects when you change your iMac's volume: On some keyboards, when you press a volume button, a sound is played so you can hear the new volume level. To stop this sound from playing, deactivate the "**Play feedback when volume is changed**" feature.

You can also have a screen flash when you receive an alert. Click on the Apple menu icon🍎, click on the **System Settings** button in the menu, and then click on the **Accessibility** button in the sidebar. Click on the **Audio** button on the right side of the window, and then activate the **"Flash the screen when alerts sound occurs"** feature.

Take a screenshot or record your iMac's screen

You can take a picture (called a screenshot) or record your iMac's display using the Screenshots feature or keyboard shortcuts. Screenshot provides a tools panel that allows you to capture screenshots & record videos easily, with options to control what you're capturing, for instance, you can add a timer delay.

Capture photos or record your screen using Screenshot

➔ Press Shift-Cmd-5 to launch the Screenshot feature & bring out the tools.
  You can also open Screenshots from Launchpad.

→ Click on one of the tools to select what you want to record or snap.

For a part of your iMac's screen, drag the frame to change its position or drag the edges to change the size of the area you plan on snapping or recording.

→ Click on the following icon to perform the actions below:

- Click the Full-Screen button to snap the whole display.

- Click the Window button to snap a window

- Click on the Section icon to snap a part of your iMac's display.

- Click on the Record Full Screen button to record the whole display.

- Click on the Record Segment button to record a part of your iMac's display.

→ If you want, click Options.

The available options vary depending on whether you are capturing the screen's content or recording your display.

The "Show Floating Thumbnail" option makes it easier to work with a finished screen recording or screenshot—it floats in the lower right corner of your display for some seconds, so you have time to drag the file into documents, markup the file, or share the file before saving it.

➔ Start recording your screen or taking screenshots:

- For the full display or a section of it: Click the **Capture** button.
- For a window: Hover your cursor to the window, and then click on the window.
- For recording: Click on the **Record** button. To stop recording, click on the Stop Recording icon⊙ on the menus bar.

With Show Floating Thumbnail, you can carry out any of the below while the thumbnail is displayed in the lower right corner of your display:

- Swipe to the right to store the file & make it disappear.
- Drag the thumbnail into an e-mail, Finder window, note, etc.
- Click on the thumbnail to open a window where you can write or draw in the picture, cut the video clip, or share the file.

Use keyboard shortcuts to take pictures of your screen

- To snap the whole display, press the Shift-Command-3 keyboard combination.
- To snap part of your display, press the Shift-Command-4 keyboard combination, and then drag the pointer to the part of your display you want to capture.
- To snap a window, press the Shift-Command-4 keyboard combination, and then press the Space bar.
- To open the Screenshot application, press the Shift-Command 5 keyboard combination.

To personalize these keyboard shortcuts, click on the Apple menu icon, click on the Systems Settings button in the menu, click on the Keyboards button on the sidebar, click on Keyboard Shortcuts on the right side of the window, and then click on Screenshots.

The screenshots are stored in .PNG format & the screen recordings are stored in .MOV format.

Use Touch ID

With the Touch ID sensor on your iMac's keyboard, you can unlock your iMac, authenticate purchases from Apple Books, Apps Store, & iTunes Store, and make online purchases with Apple Pay. You can also use Touch ID to login to 3rd-party applications.

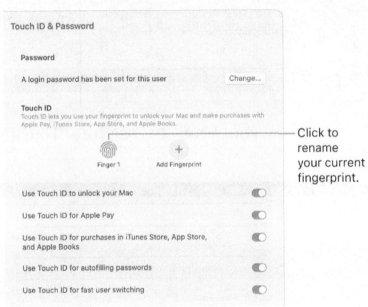

Click to rename your current fingerprint.

Setup Touch ID

→ Click on the Apple menu icon in the upper left corner of your display, click on the **Systems Settings** button in the menu, and click on the **Touch ID & Password** button on the sidebar.
→ Click the **Add Fingerprint** button, insert your passcode, and then adhere to the guidelines on your iMac's display.

You can find the Touch ID sensor close to the FN keys row in the upper right part of the keyboard. You can add up to 3 fingerprints to your user account.

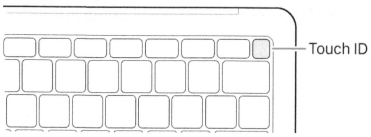

Touch ID

→ Choose how you want to use the Touch ID feature:

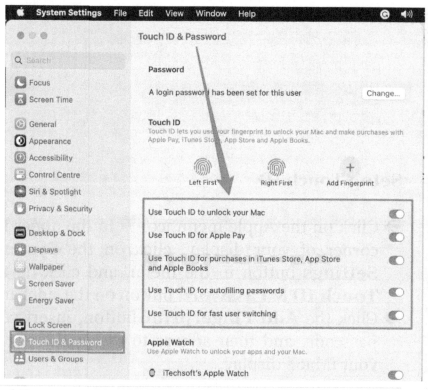

- Unlock your iMac
- Authenticate Apple Pay
- iTunes Store, Apps Store, & Apple Books.
- Quick user switching: Use Touch ID to switch from one user account to another.
- Password AutoFill: Use Touch ID to automatically fill in usernames & passcodes, and automatically fill in credit card details when prompted while making use of Safari & other applications.

Rename or delete fingerprints

➔ Click on the Apple menu icon, click on the **Systems Settings** button on the menu, and then click on the **Touch ID & Password** button on the sidebar.
➔ Carry out any of the below:
- Change the name of the fingerprint: Click on the text under a fingerprint, then type a new name.
- Delete fingerprint: Click on a fingerprint, insert your passcode, click on the **Unlock** button, and then click the **Delete** button.

Use Touch ID to unlock, sign in, or change users on your iMac

→ Unlock your iMac & some password-protected items: After waking your iMac from sleep or opening passcode-protected items, simply put your registered finger on the Touch ID sensor when told to.
→ Sign in from the sign-in window: Click on your name in the sign-in window, then put your registered finger on the Touch ID sensor.

Increase the size of everything on your display

You can change the resolution of your display to make everything on your screen appear bigger.

→ Click on the Apple menu icon, click on the **System Setting** button on the menu, and then click on Display in the side bar.
→ Select one of the resolutions on the right side of the window.
A lower resolution will increase the size of everything on your iMac's display.

Change the size of the text

➜ In applications: You can press Cmd-Plus (+) or Cmd-Minus (-) to change the text size when reading e-mails, articles, & webpages in some applications, like Mails, News, Safari, etc.

➜ In desktop labels: Ctrl-click on the desktop, click Show View Option, click on the Text Size menu, and then pick one of the text sizes.

➜ In sidebars: Click on the Apple menu icon, click on Systems Settings, and then click on the **Appearance** button in the sidebar. Click on the drop-down menu close to "sidebar icon size" on the right side of the window, and then pick **Large**.

➜ In folder & file names in the Finder: Click on View, click on Show View Option. Click on the Text Size drop-down menu, and pick one of the text sizes.

Increase the size of icons

➜ On the desktop: Ctrl-click on your desktop, click Show View Option, and then move the Icon Size slider by dragging it to the right or left.

➜ In sidebars: Click on the Apple menu icon, click on Systems Settings, and then click on the **Appearance** button in the sidebar. Click on the drop-down menu close to "Sidebar icon size" on the right side of the window, and then click on **Large**.

→ In the Finder window: Click on View, click on Show View Option. In List view & Icon view, select one of the icon sizes. You can pick a bigger thumbnail size in the Gallery view.

Use Hover Text

When you activate the Hover Text feature on your iMac, you can move the cursor over text on your iMac's display to see a zoomed version of the text in another window.

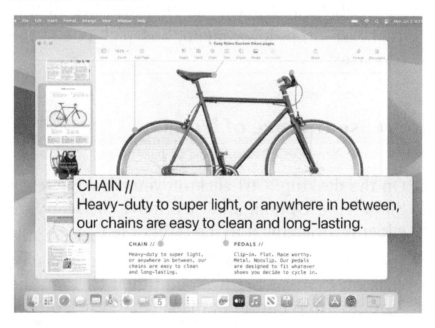

Activate & personalize Hover Text

→ Click on the Apple menu icon🍎, click on the **System Setting** button in the menu, click on Accessibility in the side bar, and then click on **Zoom** on the right side of the window.

→ Enable the **Hover Text** feature

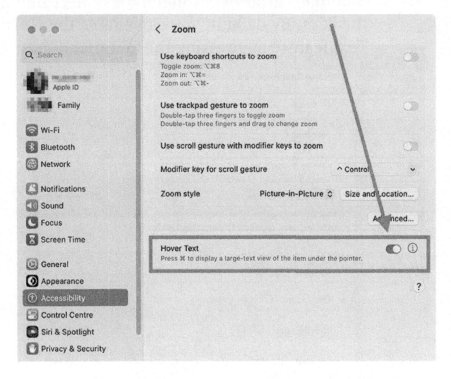

To customize the Hover Text feature, click on the Information icon🛈 beside it. For instance, you can choose:

- The window's position when you enter text. Click on the "Texts-entry location" drop-down menu and choose one of the locations. If you do not want the window to appear while you type, simply select the **None** option.
- The modifier button you press to enable the Hover Text feature. Click on the "Activation Modifier" drop-down menu and select one of the keys. By default, you can enable the Hover Text feature by pressing the Command button.

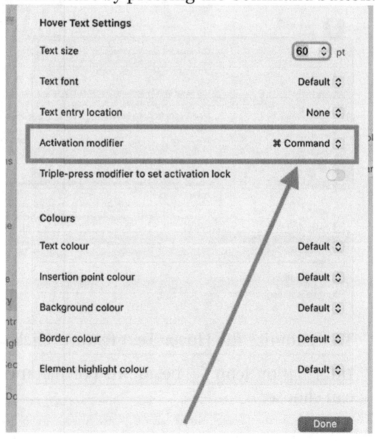

You can set Hover Text to automatically appear when you hover the cursor over an item. To do this, simply activate **Triple-press modifier to set activation lock**, then when you want the Hover Text feature to be active for a certain period — like when you are filling a form — triple-press the selected modifier key. Triple-press the modifier key again to disable the activation lock

- The colours used in the window & the text displayed in the window. Click on the drop-down menu to pick a colour or create a custom colour.

Use Hover Text

➜ Move the cursor over an item on your screen, and then press the activation modifier key (the **Command** key or the one you selected when customizing Hover text) to show the Hover Text window.

➜ If you activated the **Triple-press modifier to set activation lock** feature, press the modifier button 3 times quickly to automatically display the Hover Text window anytime you hover the cursor over an item. Triple-press the modifier key again to deactivate the activation lock

➜ If you've chosen to display the text entry window, the window will appear in the location you've specified, like the upper-left corner of your display whenever you are in a text input field. As you type, a bigger version of what is being typed will be shown in the window.

Make transparent items solid

Some windows & certain areas of your desktop, like the menus bar & the Dock, are transparent by default. You can make these areas gray so that you can easily distinguish them from the background.

→ Click the Apple menu icon, click the **System Setting** button in the menu, click on Accessibility in the sidebar, and then click on **Display** on the right side of the window.
→ Activate the **Reduce Transparency** feature.

Change the size & colour of the pointer/cursor

If you have trouble seeing or following the cursor, you can change its size & colour to make it easy to find it on your iMac's display.

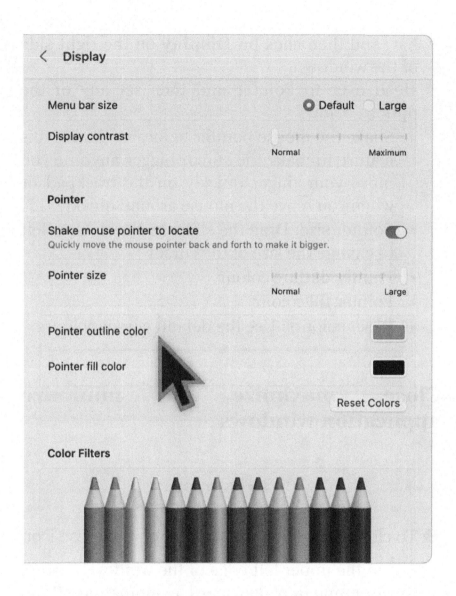

→ Click on the Apple menu icon in the upper left part of your display, click on the **System Setting** button, click on Accessibility in the side bar, and then click on **Display** on the right side of the window.

→ Head over to Pointer and then set any of the options below:

- Shake the mouse pointer to locate: Enable this feature to make the cursor bigger anytime you move your finger quickly on the trackpad or when you move the mouse around quickly.
- Pointer size: Drag the slider to the right or left to change the size of the cursor
- Pointer outline colour
- Pointer fill colour
- Reset colours: Use the default cursor colours

Close, maximize, or minimize application windows

→ To close a window, simply click on the Close icon ⓧ in the upper left edge of the window or press the Command-W keyboard combination. Press Option-Cmd-W to close all windows for an application.

→ Maximize a window: Long-press the Option button on the keyboard while clicking the green icon  on the upper left edge of a window. To go back to the window's previous size, just option-click the green icon once more

Or, double-click the application's title bar to maximize the window

→ Minimize the window: Click on the Minimize icon in the upper left edge of the window, or press the Cmd-M keyboard combination.

You can also manually change the size of some windows by dragging the edge of the window (sides, bottom, or top).

Use applications in Split View

The Split View feature allows you to work in two applications side by side simultaneously.

➔ Move the cursor over the green icon in the upper left edge of the window, then click on **Tile Window to the Right side of the Screen** or **Tile the Window to the Left Side of the Screen** from the menu that pops-up

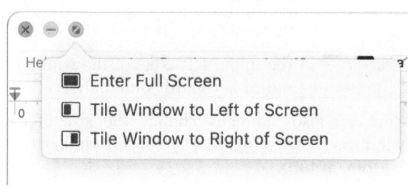

➔ On the other side of your display, click on the 2nd application you'd like to work with.
➔ Carry out any of the below in Split View:
  • Hide or display the menu bar: Hover your cursor away from or to the upper edge of your iMac's display.
  • Hide or display the Dock: Hove the cursor to or away from the location of the Dock on the screen.
  • Hide or display the toolbar & title of a window: Click on the window, then hover the cursor to or away from the upper edge of your iMac's display.
  • Increase the size of one of the windows: Hover the cursor over the center dividing bar, and

then drag it to the right or left. Double-click on the dividing bar to go back to the original size.

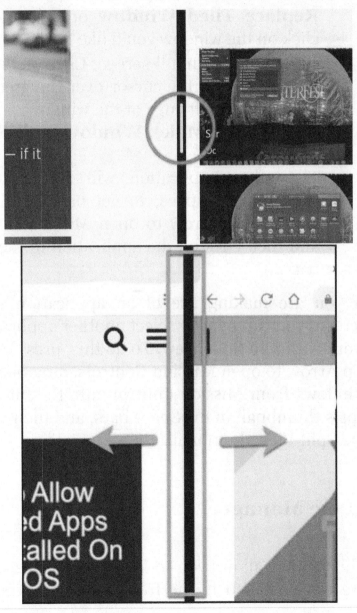

- Use another application on one side: Click on the app's window, hover the cursor over the green icon in the upper left edge, click on the **Replace Tiled Window** option, and then click on the window you'd like to use.
- Use a window in full-screen: Click on the app's window, hover the cursor over the green icon in the upper left edge of the window, and then click on the **Make Window Full-Screen** option.

    The other application will also enter full screen in its space; to get back to it, Press Control-Up Arrow to open Mission Controls, and then click on the application in the Space bars.

If you are making use of an application in full-screen, you can quickly select another application to work with it in Split View. To do this, press Control-Up Arrow to open Mission Controls, drag one of the windows from Mission Control onto the full-screen app's thumbnail in the Space bars, and then click on the Split View thumbnail.

Stage Manager

This feature allows you to keep the application you are working with in the front & center, while also making sure your desktop is clutter-free. Your recently used applications are organized on the left side of your display for fast & easy access, while the window you are using is positioned in the middle of your display.

Arrange, overlap, & change the size of windows on the layout that best suits your needs. You can also arrange multiple applications on your display to work together as a group. When you switch to the group, all the applications in the group will open in the middle of your display.

Enable or disable Stage Manager

Carry out any of the below:

→ Click on the Apple menu icon⬛ in the upper left part of your display, click on the **Systems Settings** button in the menu, and then click on Desktop & Dock⬛ in the sidebar. Head over to Desktop & Stage Manager on the right side of the window, then activate or disable Stage Manager

→ Click the Controls Centre icon⬛ in the menus bar, and then click on the Stage Manager⬛ button to activate or disable Stage Manager.

Use Stage Manager

Carry out any of the below on your iMac:

→ Switch applications: Click on one of the applications on the left side of your iMac's display.

→ Arrange Windows: Overlap, change the position & size of the windows to fit your workflow.

→ You can group applications by dragging an application from the left side of your Mac display to add it to a group of applications in the middle of the display.

→ You can ungroup applications by dragging an application to the left side of your display to remove it from the group of applications in the center of the display.

If you deactivate "**Show recent applications in Stage Manager**" in Stage Manager settings, the applications list on the left side of your display will be hidden. Hover the cursor to the left edge of your display to reveal the list.

Display or hide Stage Manager in the menu bar

You can add the Stage Manager button to the menu bar.

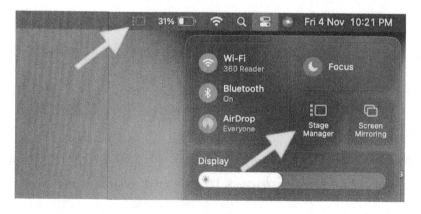

→ Click on the Apple menu icon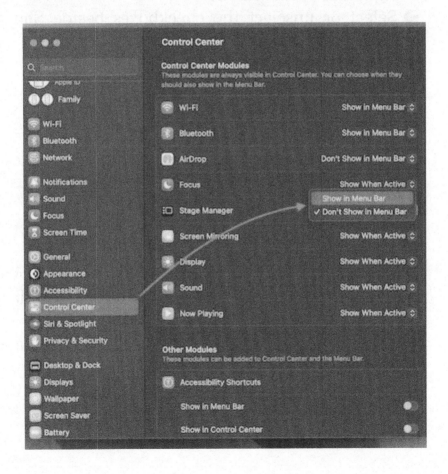 in the upper left corner of your display, click on the **Systems Settings** button in the menu, and then click on Controls Center in the sidebar on the left side of the window.

→ Click on the drop-down menu close to the Stage Manager feature on the right side of the window, and then pick one of the options.

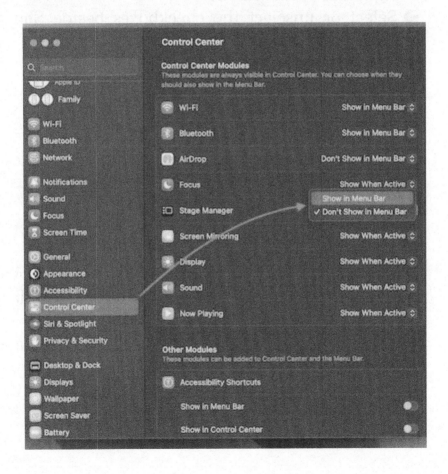

Change Stage Manager settings

→ Click on the Apple Menu icon◉ in the upper left part of your display, click on the **Systems Settings** button in the menu, and then click on Desktop & Dock⬛ in the sidebar.

→ Head over to Desktop & Stage Manager on the right side of the window

→ Select or unselect the checkboxes beside Show Items:
  - On Desktop: Display desktop items.
  - In Stage Manager: Display desktop items when the Stage Manager feature is activated. If you turn off this **option**, the items on your desktop will be hidden—click on the desktop to reveal them whenever you want to use them.

→ Click on the "Click wallpaper to reveal desktop" drop-down menu, and pick any of the options:
  - Always: Clicking on the wallpaper will move all the windows out of the way to display widgets & items.
  - Only in the Stage Manager: When Stage Manager is activated, clicking on the wallpaper will move all the windows out of the way to display widgets & items.

→ Enable or disable Stage Manager.

→ Activate or deactivate the "**Show recent applications in Stage Manager**" feature.
If this option is deactivated, recently used applications will be hidden—hover the cursor to the left edge of your display to reveal them.

→ Click on the "Show windows from an app" drop-down menu, and then pick one of the options:

- All at Once: Display all windows for an application when you switch to the application.

- One at a Time: Only display the most recently used window for an application when you switch to the application.
To switch to another window when this option is deactivated, click on the application on the left once more to open the next window.

Uninstall applications

You can delete applications that you installed on your iMac.

→ Click on the Finder icon in the Dock, and then click on the **Applications** button in the side bar.

→ Carry out any of the below:

- If the application is in a folder: Open the application's folder to see if it has an Uninstaller. If you see Uninstall [Apps] or [Apps] Uninstaller, double–click on it, and then adhere to the instructions on your display.
- If the application is not in a folder or does not have an Uninstaller, just drag the app from the Apps folder to the Trash (which can be found at the end of the Dock).

Personalize the desktop image

You can change your desktop's wallpaper. Select from the available images or colours, or use one of yours.

→ Click on the Apple menu icon in the upper left part of your display, click on the **Systems Settings** button in the menu, and then click on

Wallpapers in the side bar.
→ Choose one of the wallpapers from any of the categories:
- Add Photos/Add Folders or Albums: Controls for selecting your own photos.

- Dynamic Wallpapers: These images lighten & darken depending on the time of the day you are currently in.

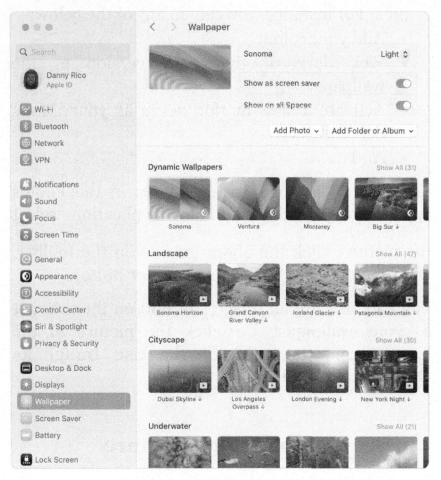

- Landscapes, Earth, Underwater, & Cityscapes aerials: These pictures show beautiful views.
- Shuffle Aerials: These pictures change at scheduled times.
- Pictures.

- Colours
→ Set options for your wallpaper.
  The options vary depending on the wallpaper you
  pick. For instance, you can do any of the below:
  - Add your colour
  - Pick dark or light still version of the
    wallpapers
  - Activate a slow-motion aerial as your iMac's
    Screensaver
  - And more

To quickly use one of your photos in the Photos
application, launch the Photos application, select
the picture, click the Share icon⬆ on the toolbar,
and then click on the **Set Wallpaper** button.

You can also use an image you find on the internet
as your wallpaper. Ctrl-click the picture in the
browser and then click on the **Use Image as
Desktop Picture** option

Change your user login picture

You can change the photo that's displayed close to
your username in the login window on your iMac.
Your user login photo is also used as your Apple ID
photo.

You can use one of your pictures, use an emoji, Memoji, or monogram, or even capture a new picture with your iMac's Camera.

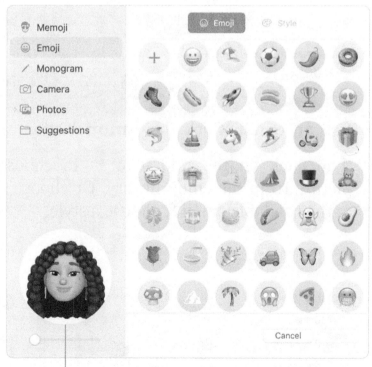

Click to change the user picture.

→ Click on the Apple menu icon in the upper left part of your display, click on the **Systems Settings** button in the menu, and then click on **Users & Group** in the side bar.

→ Click on the user photo close to your login name on the right side of the window, and then carry out any of the below:

- Use a Memoji: Click the **Memoji** option, and then click on the Add icon to pick & compose one for yourself. Or pick any of the available Memoji, then choose a style & pose.

- Use an emoji: Click the **Emoji** button, and then click on the Add icon to choose a picture from the emoji library. Or choose any of the available emoji & choose a style.

- Use a monogram: Click the **Monogram** button, choose a colour for the background, and then type your initials.

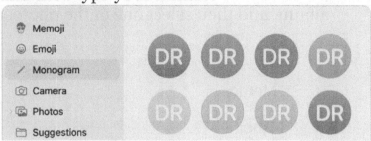

- Take a photo with your iMac's camera: Click on the **Camera** option. Get ready for the shot, and then click the Snap button. You can snap the picture as many times as needed.

- Choose one of the pictures in your Photos library: Click on the **Photos** option. To view pictures from a specific album, click on the album, and then select one of the photos.

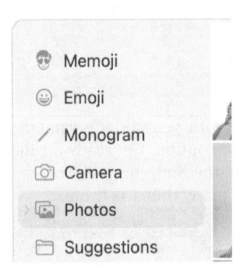

- Choose one of the recommended images: Click the **Suggestion** option, then pick any of the pictures.

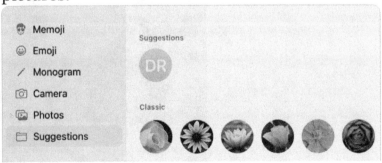

→ After choosing a picture, you can make adjustments to its appearance. Carry out any of the below:
- Adjust picture position: Drag the image inside the circle.
- Drag the slider to the right or left to zoom in or out.

→ Click the **Save** button.

Use light or dark mode

You can use a dark or light theme for the Dock, menus bar, windows, & some applications, or have it automatically change from light to dark mode during the day.

Light   Dark   Auto

→ Click on the Apple menu icon in the menu bar, click on the **Systems Setting** button, and then click on the **Appearance** button in the sidebar.

→ Select one of the options in the Appearance section on the right side of the window(Auto, Dark, or Light)

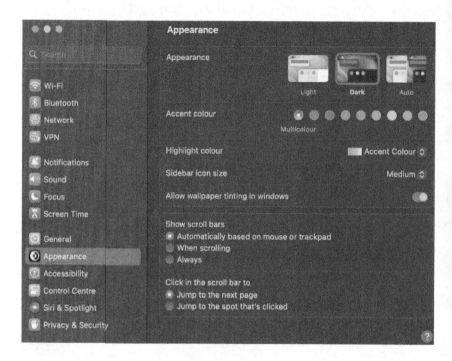

Use a screensaver

Use a screensaver to hide your desktop when you are away from your iMac or if you need more privacy.

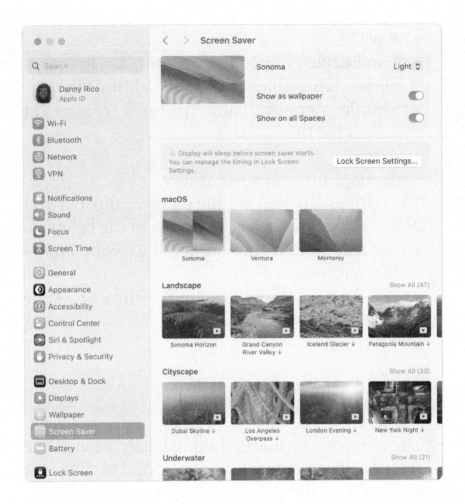

Personalize the screen saver

→ Click on the Apple menu icon in the menu bar, click on the **Systems Setting** button, and then click on the **Screen Saver** button in the sidebar.

→ Click on one of the screensavers from any of the available categories:

- macOS
- Landscapes, Earth, Underwater, & Cityscapes aerials: These pictures show beautiful views.
- Shuffle Aerials: These pictures change at scheduled times.
- Other

➔ Set options for your screensaver.

The options vary depending on the wallpaper you pick. For instance, you can do any of the below:

- Activate a slow-motion aerial as your iMac's Screensaver
- Select a pattern to shuffle through your pictures
- And more

Start or stop the screensaver

➔ The screensaver starts automatically when your iMac has been inactive for the period of time you selected in settings.

To change how long your iMac has to stay idle before the screensaver activates, click on the Apple menu icon in the upper left part of your display, click on the **Systems Settings** button in the menu, and then click on the **Lock Screen** button in the side bar & select settings on the right side of the window.

→ Tap the trackpad, move the mouse, or press a key on the keyboard to stop the screensaver & display your desktop.

Require a password after waking your device

To keep your data safe when you're away from your iMac, set your device to require a login code when it wakes from sleep.

→ Click on the Apple menu icon🍎, click on the **Systems Setting** button in the menu, and then click on the **Lock Screen** button in the sidebar.
→ Click on the drop-down menu close to "Require a password after screensaver starts or screen is turned off," then select the amount of time that has to pass before the password is needed.

Change Lock Screen settings

Use the Lock Screen settings to protect your iMac from tampering & malware.

To change these settings, click on the Apple menu icon🍎 in the upper left part of your display, click on the **Systems Setting** button in the menu, click on the **Lock Screen**  button in the sidebar, and then select any of the options on the right side of the window and make the needed changes.

Use Hot Corners

The Hot Corners feature allows you to start a quick action when you hover the cursor to one of the corners of your iMac's display. For instance, you can lock your screen when you hover the cursor to the upper right corner of your iMac's display

→ Click on the Apple Menu icon in the upper left part of your display, click on the **Systems Setting** button in the menu, and then click on the **Desktop and Dock** button in the sidebar.
→ Click on the **Hot Corners** button on the right side of the window.

→ Click on the drop-down menu for each corner you want to use, and then pick one of the options, like Lock Screen, Launchpad, etc.

→ Click on Done

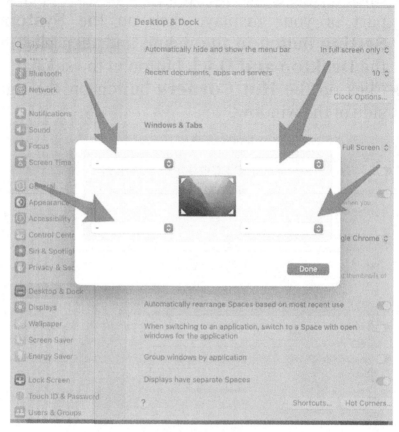

Use Night Shift

Use the Night Shift feature to change the colours on the screen to the warmer side of the colour spectrum. Warm screen colours are more pleasant to look at at night or in low-light conditions. In addition, exposure to blue light in the evening can make it difficult to fall asleep.

Set Night Shift to activate or deactivate automatically

→ Click on the Apple menu icon 🍎 in the upper left part of your display, and then click on the **Systems Setting** button in the menu.

→ Click on the **Display** 🔆 button in the side bar

→ Click on **Night Shift** on the right side of the window, click on the Schedule drop-down menu, and select one of the options.

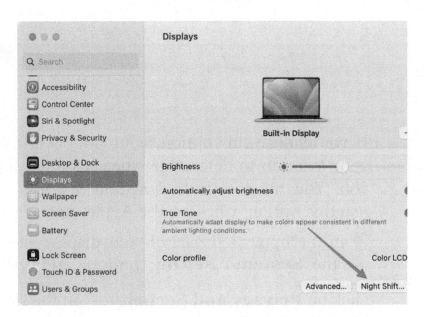

- Off

- Custom: Set the times you want the Night Shift to be activated & deactivated.
- Sunset to Sunrise: Use the Night Shift feature from sunset to sunrise.

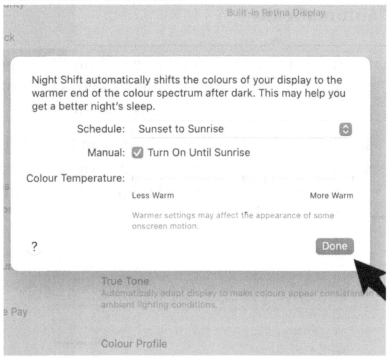

If you choose this option, your iMac will use your location to determine when it's night for you. You must activate Location Services to use this option. Click on the Apple menu icon in the upper left part of your display, click on the **Systems Setting** button, and then click on **Privacy and Security** in the side bar. Click on Location Services on the right side of the window, and then activate the Location Services feature. Scroll to Systems Service, click on the **Details** button, activate Setting time zone, and then click on Done.

Activate & deactivate Night Shift

You can enable or disable Night Shift whenever you want, for instance, if you are in a dark room.

→ Click on the Apple menu icon in the upper left part of your display, and then click on the **Systems Setting** button in the menu.

→ Click on the **Display** button in the side bar
→ Click on **Night Shift** on the right side of the window, and then activate the **Turn on till tomorrow** feature.
Night Shift will remain active till the following day or till you deactivate it.

Tip: You can also enable or deactivate Night Shift through the Controls Centre. Click on the Controls Centre icon in the menu bar, click on Display, and then click on the **Night Shift** button.

Adjust the colour temperature

→ Click on the Apple menu icon in the upper left part of your display, and then click on the **Systems Setting** button in the menu.

→ Click on the **Display** button in the side bar

→ Click on **Night Shift** on the right side of the window, and then drag the slider to the right or left to adjust the colour temperature used by Night Shift.

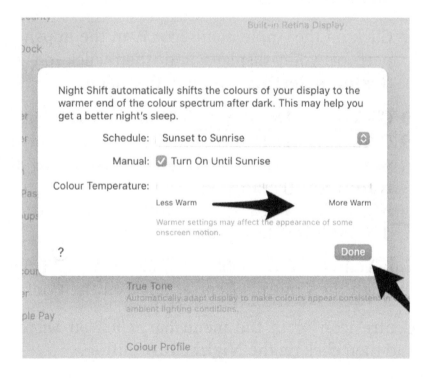

Change your iMac's language

➔ Click on the Apple menu icon in the upper left part of your display, and then click on the **Systems Setting** button in the menu.

➔ Click on the **General** button in the sidebar, then click on Language and Region on the right side of the window.

➔ In the Preferred Languages segment, click on the Add icon , pick any of the languages in the List, and then click on the **Add** button.

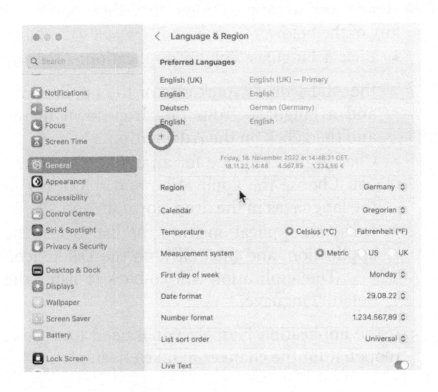

Select the language you use for each app

→ Click on the Apple menu icon in the upper left part of your display, click on the **Systems Setting** button in the menu, click on the **General** button in the sidebar, and then click on Language and Region on the right side of the window.
→ Head over to Applications, and then carry out any of the below:
  • Pick a language for an application: Click on the Add icon ┼ , pick one of the applications and a language from the drop-down menu, and then click on the **Add** button.
  • Change the language for an application in the list: Choose the application and select any of the languages in the drop-down menu.
  • Erase an application from the list: Select the application, and then click on the Delete icon ─── . The application will go back to using the default language.

If the application is open, you'll need to close & reopen it for the changes to take effect.

Use desktop stacks

Desktop Stacks helps to organize your files into groups on your desktop. Whenever you save a file to your desktop, it'll be automatically added to the right stack.

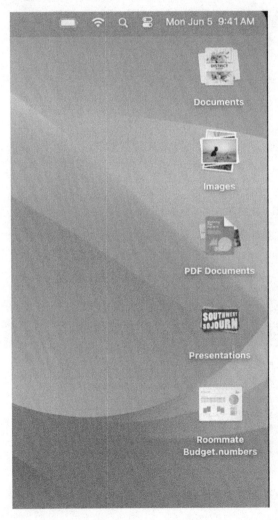

Activate desktop stacks

Carry out any of the below:

➔ Ctrl-click the desktop, then click on the **Use Stack** button in the menu

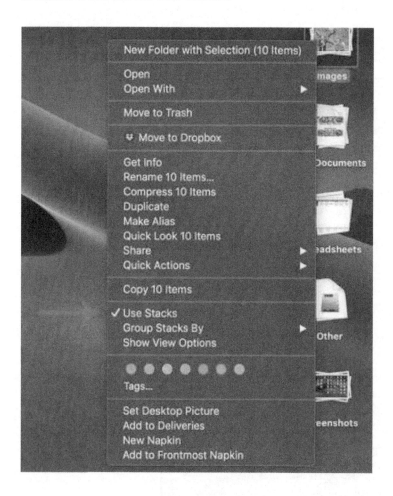

➔ Press Control-Command-0.

→ Click the desktop, click on View, and then click on the **Use Stacks** button in the menu.

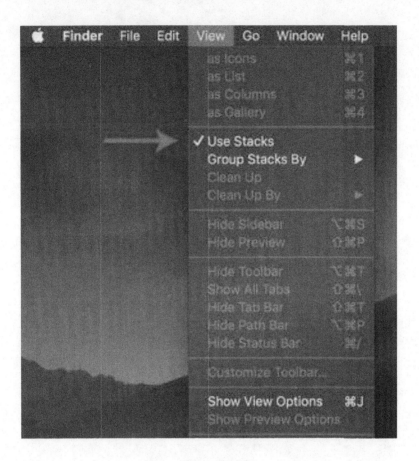

Browse files in desktop stacks

Carry out any of the below on the stack:

→ Use 2 of your fingers to swipe right or left on the trackpad.

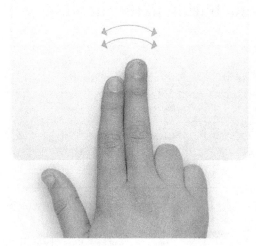

➜ Use a finger to swipe right or left on your Magic mouse

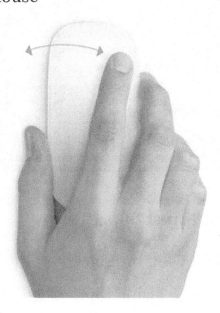

Expand or collapse desktop stacks

Carry out any of the below on your iMac:

→ Expand a desktop stack: Click on the stack on your desktop. After expanding the stack, double-click any of the items in the stack to open it.
→ You can close a desktop stack by clicking on its Down Arrow

Change the grouping of desktop stacks

You can group stacks by kind (like PDFs or pictures), date, or Finder tag.

To do this, simply carry out any of the below:

→ Click the desktop, click on View, select **Group Stacks By** in the menu, and then click on one of the options.

→ Ctrl-click on the desktop, select **Group Stacks By** in the menu, and then click on one of the options.

Change the desktop stack appearance

You can increase the size of icons, change the spacing between icons, etc.

To do this, simply carry out any of the below:

→ Click on the desktop, click on View, click on Show View Options in the menu, and then make the needed changes.

→ Ctrl-click on the desktop, click on the **Show View Options** button in the menu, then make the needed changes.

Dictation

You can dictate text anywhere you can type it on your iMac.

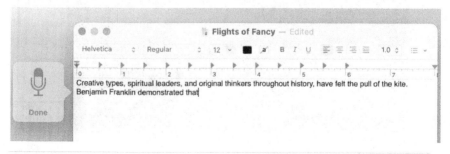

Enable or disable the Dictation feature

➜ Click on the Apple menu icon in the upper left part of your display, click on the **System Settings** button in the menu, and then click on the **Keyboard** button on the sidebar

➜ Head over to Dictation on the right side of the window, and then enable or disable it. If prompted, click on **Enable**.

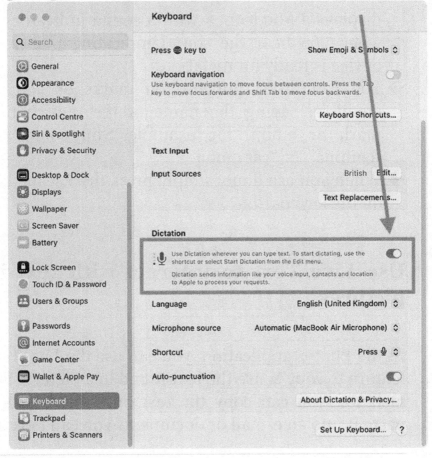

Dictate text

➜ In an application that supports text editing on your iMac, place the insertion point where you want to enter text.

➜ Press the Dictation key in the Fn row on your keyboard, or click on Edit, and then click on the **Start Dictation** button

➜ Start dictating when the feed-back window displays a Mic icon with a sound indicator, or when you hear the sound indicating that your device is ready for dictation.

➜ You can insert punctuation marks or add an emoji by saying the name of the punctuation mark or emoji, for example, you could say "comma" or "car emoji"

➜ When you are done, simply press the Escape key on the keyboard.

Use Live Text to interact with text in pictures

In the Photos application, you can use the Live Text feature to copy & use the text found in a picture. For instance, you can copy the text on a signboard & paste it into an e-mail or document. You can look up word definitions, search the web, and even translate text into another language. If a picture displays a phone number, e-mail address, or website, you can use it to start a call, compose an e-mail, or visit a site.

→ In the Photos application, open a picture that has text in it.

→ Hover the cursor over the text, and then drag to select the text.

→ Carry out any of the below:

- Copy text: Press the Command-C keyboard shortcut or Ctrl-click on the text you've selected, and then click on the **Copy** button.

- Translate text: Ctrl-click on what you've selected, select Translate [text], and then select one of the languages.

- Check the meaning of a word: Ctrl-click on what you've selected, and then click on Lookup [text].

- Share the text: Ctrl-click on what you've selected, click on Share, then select one of the sharing options.

- Search for the text on the Internet: Ctrl-click on what you've selected, and then click on Search with [web searching engine].

- Go to a site: Ctrl-click on what you've selected, then open the link in a browser.

- Contact an e-mail address: Ctrl-click on what you've selected, and then choose to write an e-mail or add the e-mail address to your Contacts list.

- Contact a phone number: Ctrl-click on what you've selected, and then choose to call the phone number, start a Face-Time call, or send a message to the phone number.

Add users on your iMac

If you have multiple users on your iMac, you need to create accounts for each individual so that each person can adjust settings and options without affecting the other users. You must be an administrator on your iMac to perform these tasks.

➔ On your iMac, click on the Apple menu icon in the upper left part of your display, and then click on the **Systems Setting** button in the menu.
➔ Click on Users & Groups on the sidebar, and click on the Add Users button under the Users list on the right side of the window (you may be told to insert your password.)
➔ Click on the New User drop-down menu, and select a user type.
- Administrator: Administrators can add and manage other users, install applications, and adjust settings. The new user you create the first time you setup your iMac is an administrator. You can decide to have multiple administrators on your Mac.

- Standard: Standard users can install applications and make changes to their own settings, but they cannot add other users.
- Shared only: Shared-only users can remotely access shared files, but cannot sign in to your device or make changes to the settings.

➜ Type the name of the user. The account name will be generated automatically. If you don't like the account name, change it now— you cannot change it later.

➜ Type a passcode for the new user, and then type the password one more time to confirm. Type a hint for the passcode to help the new user remember their passcode.

➜ Click the **Create User** button.

➜ If you want, customize what this user can do. Click the Details icon ⓘ beside the username, and then carry out any of the below:

- Select the "**Allow users to reset passwords with Apple ID**" option. To use this option, the user must have setup iCloud on this iMac.
- To make a standard user an administrator, activate the "**Allow this user to administer this Mac**" feature.

Quick Note

With the Quick Note feature, you can write down thoughts no matter what you are doing on your iMac. The Quick Note will remain visible on your iMac's display when it's open, so you can easily select & add info.

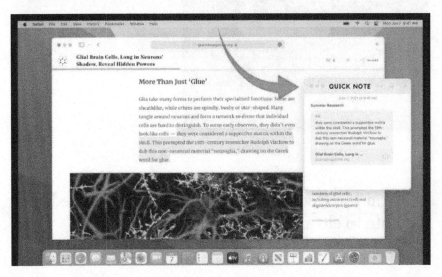

Start a Quick Note

Do any of the below to open a Quick Note:

→ Hold down the Function button or Globe button , and then press Q.

→ Use hot corners: Hover the cursor to the lower right edge of your display, and then click on the note that pops-up.

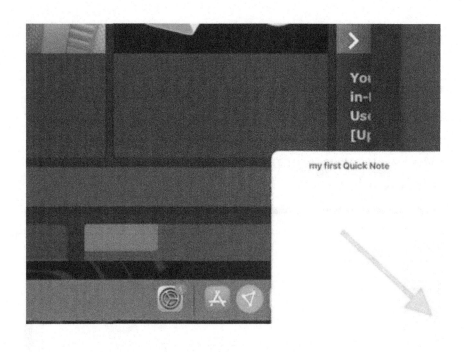

Click on the Red button ⊗ in the upper left edge of the note to close it

Control access to your iMac's camera

Some applications you install can use your iMac's camera to capture videos & pictures. You can choose the applications that are allowed to access your camera.

→ Click on the Apple menu icon in the upper left corner of the screen, click on the **System**

Settings button in the menu, and then click on

the **Privacy and Security** 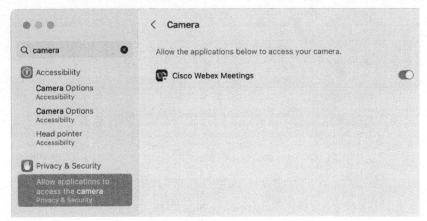 button in the sidebar

➔ Click on Camera on the right side of the window.

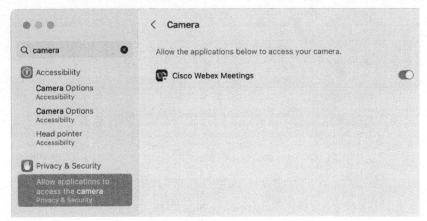

➔ Activate or disable access to your iMac's camera for each application in that section.

Change password or user photo

➔ Click on the Apple menu icon in the upper left corner of your display, click on the **System Settings** button in the menu, and then click on the **User and Group** button on the sidebar

➔ Click on the Information icon beside a user in the list on the right side of the window, and then carry out any of the below:

- Click Change Password or Reset Password.
- Click a user's photo to change the login photo

Optimize storage space

MacOS can help you free up more space on your iMac by optimizing storage.

→ Click on the Apple menu icon in the upper left corner of your display, click on the **System Settings** button in the menu, and then click on the **General** button on the sidebar

➔ Click on **Storage** on the right side of the window

Recommendations

Store in iCloud   Store in iCloud...
Store all files, photos, and messages in iCloud and
save space by keeping only recent files and
optimized photos on this Mac when storage space is
needed. Learn more...

Optimize Storage   Optimize...
Save space by automatically removing movies and TV
shows that you've already watched from this Mac.

Empty Trash automatically   Turn On...
Save space by automatically erasing items that have been in
the Trash for more than 30 days. Learn more...

➔ Check out what macOS is recommending and decide how to optimize storage

- Store in iCloud

  Store in iCloud
  Store all files, photos, and messages in iCloud and
  save space by keeping only recent files and
  optimized photos on this Mac when storage space is
  needed. Learn more...

- Optimize Storage

  Optimize Storage
  Save space by automatically removing movies and TV
  shows that you've already watched from this Mac.

- Empty Trash automatically

Empty Trash automatically
Save space by automatically erasing items that have been in the Trash for more than 30 days. Learn more...

Music on iMac

The Music application makes organizing & enjoying music easy on your iMac. You can check out previously played songs, lyrics for what is playing, & what is next. You can also purchase your favorite music from the iTunes Store.

Your library: You can find & play songs you purchased from the iTunes Store, music you added from the Apple Music catalogue, and songs from your library. You can filter content by Songs, Albums, Artists, or Recently Added.

Check out the best of Apple Music. Click on the **Browse** button in the sidebar on the left part of the window to check out the latest songs & exclusive releases from Apple Music (a streaming service that's accessible for a monthly fee). Stream & download songs ads-free & select from dozens of playlists to find the ideal mix every time. You can even follow an artist to get new songs alerts.

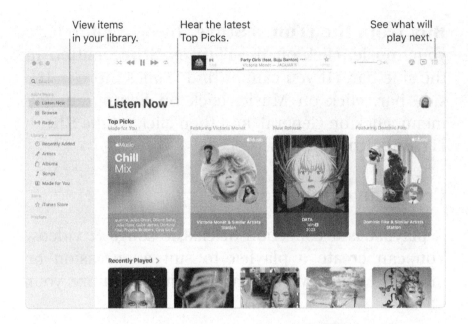

View items in your library.

Hear the latest Top Picks.

See what will play next.

Lyrics: Click on the Lyrics button 💬 in the tool bar to see a lyrics panel for the song that is playing (if available).

Listen together: With the Shareplay feature, you can listen to songs in real-time with other people. Firstly, bring the group together in a Face-Time call, and then click on the SharePlay button 👥. To listen to songs together, hover the cursor over an album or song in the Music application, then click on Play. Every participant in the Face-Time call will be able to hear the same song at the same time, & have access to shared playback controls.

Buy from the iTunes Store. If you want to have your music, click on the **iTunes Store** button in the side bar. (If you cannot find iTunes Store in the side bar, click on Music, click on Settings in the menu, click on General, and then click on the **Show iTunes Store** button.)

Create an empty Playlist

A playlist is a collection of classic songs & videos. You can create a playlist to suit an occasion or mood, to share with friends, or just organize your library

Adhere to the directives below to create a playlist:

➔ In the Music application, click on File, click on New, and then click on Playlist

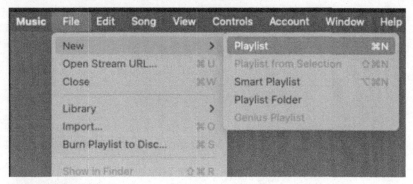

The Playlist you just created will appear in the side bar under Playlists.

➔ Give the playlist a name

Add items to the playlist

➔ In the Music application, click on Browse, Listen Now, or any of the other options in the Library segment on the side bar to find the songs you want to add to the playlist.

➔ To add an item to a playlist, carry out any of the below:

- Ctrl-click on an item, click on the **Add to Playlist** button and then click on one of the playlists.

- Drag an item from anywhere in your music library to one of the playlists in the sidebar.

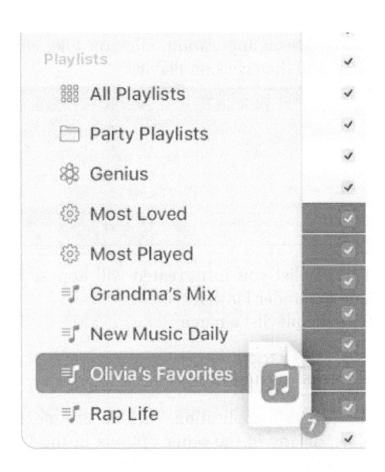

Create a playlist of songs

→ In the Music application, click on Browse, Listen Now, or any of the other options in the Library segment on the side bar to find the songs you want to add to the playlist.

→ Select one or more songs, control-click, click on Add to Playlists, and then click on the **New Playlist** button

The Playlist you just created will appear in the side bar under Playlists.

Edit a playlist

➜ Select one of the playlists in the sidebar.
➜ Carry out any of the below:
  • Change the songs' order: Click View> Sort By. After clicking View> Sort By> Playlists Order, simply drag & drop the songs to rearrange them.
  • Change the name of the playlist: Select the name of the playlist in the upper part of the window, and then type another name.
  • Delete a song from your playlist: Select the song, and then press the **Delete** button on the keyboard.

Delete a playlist

➜ Carry out any of the below in the Music application:
  • Select one of the playlists in the side bar, and then press the **Delete** button on the keyboard.
  • Ctrl-click the playlist in the sidebar, and then click on the **Delete from Library** button.
➜ Click on **Delete** once more.

See which playlist a song is in

→ In the Apple Music application, click on the **Songs** button in the sidebar.

→ Ctrl-click on a song, and then click on the **Show in Playlist** button.

The submenu will display which library & playlist category the song is in. Select the playlist from the submenu to open it.

Use AirDrop

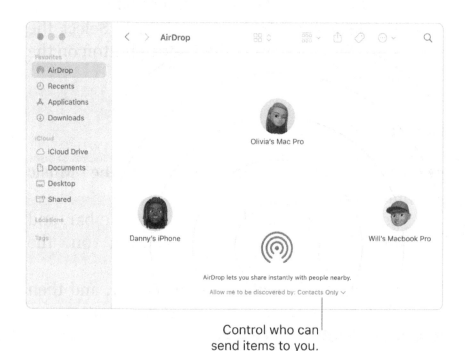

Control who can send items to you.

You can use AirDrop as a means to share files with Apple devices that are close to you (iPad, iPhone, & Mac).

Send a file from the Finder. Ctrl-click on the item you'd like to share, click on Share from the shortcut menu, click on the **AirDrop** button, and then choose the device you'd like to send the file to. Or open Finder, and then click the **AirDrop** button in the side bar. When the device you want to share the file with pops up in the window, simply drag the file to it.

Send files from an application. While making use of applications like Preview or Pages, click on the Share icon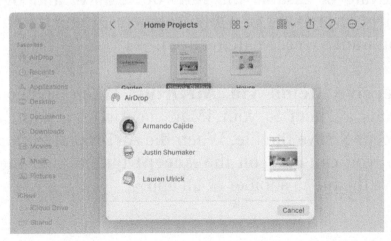 in the application's toolbar, click on the **AirDrop** option, and then choose the device you'd like to share the file with.

Use Controls Centre to manage AirDrop

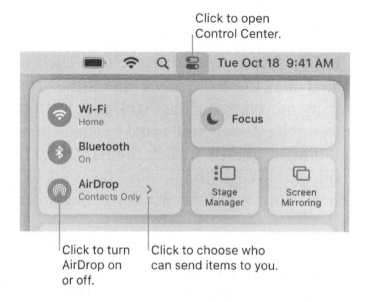

Click to open
Control Center.

Tue Oct 18 9:41 AM

Wi-Fi
Home

Bluetooth
On

AirDrop
Contacts Only

Focus

Stage
Manager

Screen
Mirroring

Click to turn
AirDrop on
or off.

Click to choose who
can send items to you.

Click the Controls Centre icon in the right part of the menu bar, click on the **AirDrop** button to activate or disable the AirDrop feature, and then select Everybody or Only Contacts to choose who you want to receive items from.

Receive items via AirDrop: When someone sends an item to your iMac via AirDrop, you can accept & save the file. When the AirDrop alert pops up, you can click on the **Accept** button, and then save the file to a folder or an app.

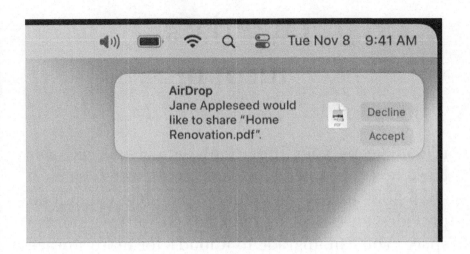

CHAPTER 5

ICLOUD

iCloud keeps your important data, (such as your back ups, documents, videos, & pictures) safe, & accessible across all your Apple devices. iCloud provides an e-mail account & 5GB of free storage space. You can upgrade to iCloud+ for more storage & features.

To begin, simply sign in with your Apple ID to setup iCloud. After signing in, basic iCloud features such as iCloud Drive, iCloud Photos, etc. are automatically configured. You can enable or disable these features & personalize the settings at any time.

Here are some ways to use iCloud on your iMac:

- → ICloud Photos keeps your videos & pictures safe and allows you to easily access the videos & pictures on all your devices & the iCloud.com site.
- → Keep your files safe & organized in iCloud Drive.
- → With the Family Sharing feature, you can share applications, books, songs, subscriptions, etc. with your family members
- → The Hide My E-mail feature keeps your e-mail address private by creating random & unique addresses that are forwarded to your personal inbox so you don't have to share your real e-mail address when filling out forms online or registering for newsletters.
- → ICloud Private Relay: Hide your IP address & browsing activities in the Safari app & encrypt your Internet traffic so that nobody, including Apple, can know who you are or what websites you're visiting.
- → iCloud Keychain: Keep your passcodes, credit cards, etc. safe in iCloud.
- → And more.

Manage iCloud storage

You get 5GB of free storage after signing in with your Apple ID & activating iCloud. If you're running out of storage space, simply upgrade to iCloud+ to increase your storage space

→ Click on the Apple menu icon in the upper left corner of your display, click on the **System Settings** button in the menu, and then click on [your name] in the upper part of the side bar. If you can't find your name, click on **Sign in to your Apple ID** to enter your Apple ID details or create one for yourself.

→ Click on **iCloud** on the right side of the window, click on the **Manage** button, and then carry out any of the below:

‹   iCloud

iCloud+   33.51 GB of 50 GB used

16.5 GB

Photos and Videos ● Backups ● Documents

Account Storage   Manage...

Optimize Mac Storage
The full contents of iCloud Drive will be stored on this Mac if you have
enough space. Older documents will be stored only in iCloud when space is
needed.

Apps Using iCloud

🌸 Photos   On ›

☁️ iCloud Drive   On ›

✉️ iCloud Mail   On ›

🔑 Password & Keychain   On ›

Show All

- Upgrade your storage space: click on Change your Storage Plan or Add Storage, then adhere to the guidelines on your screen.

- Share iCloud+ with family: If you've subscribed to iCloud+, click on the **Share with Family** button, and then adhere to the directives on your display.
- See how apps or features are using storage: Click on a feature or application in the list.
- Remove an iPad or iPhone's backup: Click on the **Backups** button in the list, select the device, and then click on Remove ▬ in the backups list section.

- Deactivate Siri & delete Siri-related data: Click the Siri option in the list, and then click on Disable & Delete
→ Click on Done.

Keep files in iCloud Drive

Keep your files safe & organized in iCloud Drive.

Set up iCloud Drive

If you haven't setup iCloud Drive yet, simply adhere to the directives below:

→ Click on the Apple menu icon in the upper left corner of your display, click on the **System Settings** button in the menu, and then click on [your name] in the upper part of the side bar. If you can't find your name, click on **Sign in to your Apple ID** to enter your Apple ID details or create one for yourself.
→ Click on **iCloud** on the right side of the window, click on the **iCloud Drive** option, and then activate Sync this Mac.
If you don't see Sync this Mac, click on Turn On.
→ Click on the **Done** button.

Keep your Desktop & Documents folders in iCloud Drive

You can automatically save all files in your Documents & Desktop folders to iCloud Drive. So you can save files wherever you usually save them, and they'll be accessible on all your devices & iCloud.com.

→ Click on the Apple menu icon in the upper left corner of your display, click on the **System Settings** button in the menu, and then click on [your name] in the upper part of the side bar. If you can't find your name, click on **Sign in to your Apple ID** to enter your Apple ID details or create one for yourself.

→ Click on **iCloud** on the right side of the window, click on the **iCloud Drive** option, then ensure iCloud Drive is activated.

→ Activate Desktop and Document Folders

→ Click on the **Done** button.

After activating Desktop and Document Folders, the Desktop & Document folders will be moved to iCloud Drive. It's also available in the iCloud segment of the Finder side bar

Use iCloud Photos

When you activate iCloud Photos, all your videos & pictures in the Photos library will be saved in iCloud, so you can easily gain access to the files on your other devices (PC, Apple TV, iPad, iPhone, iMac, MacBook, etc.) & iCloud. com.

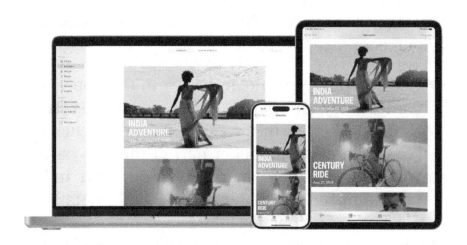

Any new videos & pictures that are added to the Photos application will appear on all your devices that have iCloud Photos enabled.

Getting Started

Do the following before setting up iCloud Photos:

→ Ensure your iMac & other devices have been updated to the latest OS(operating system like macOS, iOS, etc.) versions

→ Login with your Apple ID: If you haven't logged in with your Apple ID, Click on the Apple menu icon in the upper left corner of your display, click on the **System Settings** button in the menu, then click on **Sign in to Apple ID** in the upper part of the side bar to enter your Apple ID details or create one for yourself. Click on the **iCloud** option on the right side of the window, click on the **iCloud Photos** option in the applications list, and then activate Sync Mac.

Activate iCloud Photos

→ In the Photos application, click on Photos, click on Settings, and then click on iCloud.
→ Tick the iCloud Photo check box

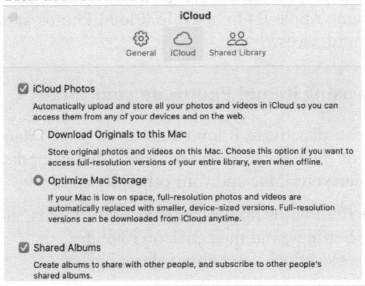

➜ Select any of the options below:
- Optimize this iMac's Storage

> ○ Optimize Mac Storage
>
> If your Mac is low on space, full-resolution photos and videos are automatically replaced with smaller, device-sized versions. Full-resolution versions can be downloaded from iCloud anytime.

- Download Originals to iMac

> Download Originals to this Mac
>
> Store original photos and videos on this Mac. Choose this option if you want to access full-resolution versions of your entire library, even when offline.

The first time you activate iCloud Photos, it may take some time to upload your pictures to iCloud. You can continue using the Photos applications while your files are being uploaded.

To sync iCloud photos across all your devices, use the same Apple ID to activate iCloud Photos across all your devices.

Stop using iCloud Photos on your iMac

You can deactivate iCloud Photos on your iMac to prevent videos & pictures from being updated between your iMac and your other devices.

➜ In the Photos application, click on Photos, click on Settings, and then click on iCloud.
➜ Unselect the iCloud Photo check box

➜ Click on the **Download** button to download videos & pictures from iCloud to your iMac, or click on the **Remove from Mac** option to remove files that haven't been fully downloaded.

After deactivating iCloud Photo on your iMac, your photos library will remain in iCloud & available to your other devices using iCloud Photos.

Stop using iCloud Photos on all your Apple devices

➜ Click on the Apple menu icon in the upper left corner of your display, click on the **System Settings** button in the menu, and then click on [your name] in the upper part of the sidebar
If you do not see your name, simply click on **Sign in to Apple ID** in the upper part of the side bar to enter your Apple ID details or create one for yourself.
➜ Click on the **iCloud** option on the right side of the window
➜ Click on the Manage option, click on Photos, and then click on **"Turn Off & Delete"**

NOTE: If you deactivate iCloud Photos on all your devices, your files will be deleted from iCloud after 30 days, and you will not be able to get them back unless you click on the **Undo Delete** button before that time.

CHAPTER 6

SIRI

Use Siri to perform everyday tasks, such as scheduling meetings, launching applications, or getting answers to questions on your iMac.

Click to close
the Siri window.

Click the Siri icon,
then make a request.

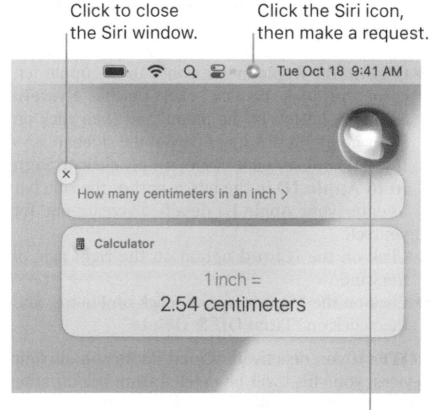

Click to make
another request.

Activate Siri

➔ Click on the Apple menu icon in the upper left part of your display, and then click on the **System Settings** button in the menu.

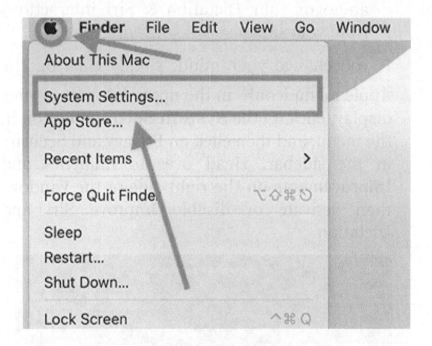

➔ Click on the Siri & Spotlight button in the side bar, enable the Ask Siri feature on the right side of the window if you haven't, then click on Enable

Your iMac has to be connected to the Internet before you can use Siri.

➔ When asked if you'd like to improve Siri & Dictation, simply do any of the below:
- Click on the **Not Now** option to not share your voice recordings
- Share voice recordings: Click on the **Share Audio Recordings** button to let Apple keep audio of your Dictation & Siri interactions from your iMac.

If you change your mind, simply click on the Apple menu icon in the upper left part of your display, click on the **System Settings** button in the menu, and then click on Privacy and Security in the sidebar. Head over to Analytics and Improvements on the right side of the window, then activate or disable Improve Siri and Dictation.

➔ Carry out any of the below:
- Use "Siri" or "Hey Siri": Activate the "Listen for" feature or select a phrase you'd like to say to activate Siri. When this option is enabled

and you activate the "**Allow Siri when locked**" feature, you can also summon Siri even when your iMac is locked.

- Create a shortcut: Click on the "Keyboard Shortcut" drop-down menu, and then pick one of the shortcuts to activate Siri or create one for yourself.

Tip: You can hold down the microphone button 🎤 in the FN keys row on your keyboard to activate Siri.

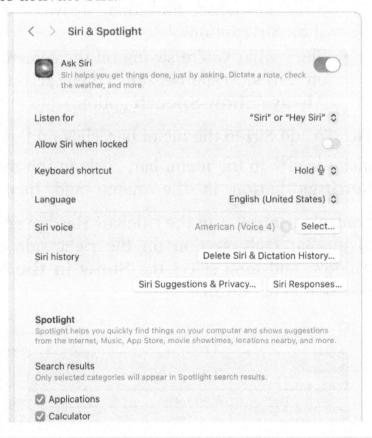

- Change Siri's Voice or Language: Click on the Language drop-down menu, and then pick one of the languages. To hear a preview of Siri's voice, click on the Select button beside **Siri Voice**, and then pick any of the available Voice Varieties & options
- Mute Siri: Click on Siri's Response, and then deactivate the **Voice feedback**— you'll see Siri's response in the Siri window.
- See Siri's Response on your display: Click on Siri's Response, and then activate "Always show Siri captions."
- Show what you're saying on the screen: Click on Siri's Response, and then activate the **Always Show Speech** option.

Tip: To add Siri to the menu bar, click on the Apple menu icon in the menu bar, click on the **System Settings** button in the menu, and then click Controls Centre in the sidebar. Head over to the Menu Bar Only section on the right side of the window, and then select the **Show in the Menu Bar** option beside Siri.

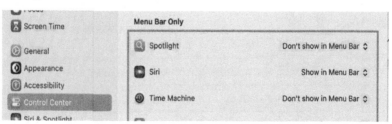

Summon Siri

Your iMac has to have internet connection before you can use Siri.

➔ Carry out any of the below to summon Siri:

- Hold down the Microphone key in the FN keys row on your keyboard or use the keyboard shortcut you created.
- Click on the Siri button in the menu bar.
- Say "Siri" or "Hey Siri" if you've activated the **"Listen for"** feature

➔ Request for something—for instance, ask Siri to set a meeting at 10 or ask for a weather report

Deactivate Siri

➔ Click on the Apple menu icon in the upper left part of your display, and then click on the **System Settings** button in the menu

➔ Click the Siri & Spotlight button in the side bar, deactivate the Ask Siri feature on the right side of the window

CHAPTER 7

SAFARI

You can use the Safari browser to surf through the web, visit sites, translate webpages, etc.

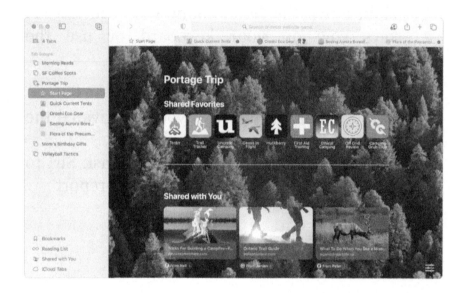

Visit a site

With the Safari app, you can easily gain access to any website.

Enter a website's name or URL.

→ Type the URL or name of the site in the search bar.
Suggestions will appear as you type.

Type what you're looking for.

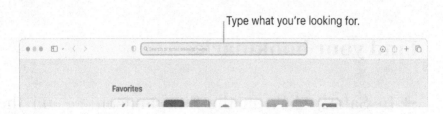

→ Choose any of the suggestions or press the Return key on the keyboard to visit the address you typed.

Add a bookmark

Bookmarks are links to sites that you save so you can quickly visit them later.

→ Visit the site you'd like to bookmark.

→ Click on the Share icon ⬆️ in the tool bar, and then click on the **Add Bookmark** button.

→ Pick where you want to add the bookmark & change the bookmark's name if you want.

- Add this page: Click on the drop-down menu and click on one of the folders.

- Change the bookmark's name: Type a short name to help identify the site.

- Add description: Type more info about the site as an additional reminder.

➜ Click on **Add**.

Find your bookmarks

➜ In Safari, click on the Sidebar icon on the toolbar, and then click on the **Bookmarks** button.

➜ Type the name of the bookmark in the search box in the upper part of the sidebar.
Scroll to bring out the search box

Use a bookmark

➜ In Safari, click the Sidebar icon on the toolbar, and then click on the **Bookmarks** button.

➜ Click on one of the bookmarks in the sidebar.

Manage bookmarks

➜ Click on the Sidebar icon on the toolbar, and then click on the **Bookmarks** button.

➜ Ctrl-click on one of the bookmarks or folders

➔ Pick from the shortcut menu to do any of the below:
- Change the name of or edit a folder or bookmark.
- Create a bookmark folder
- Make changes to the site address (URL) of the bookmark.
- Delete or copy a folder or bookmark.

To change the description of a bookmark, double-click a folder on the side bar, then ctrl-click on the item, and then click on the **Edit Descriptions** button.

Use tabs

Avoid cluttering your desktop with many windows when you are browsing or researching a topic online. Instead, you can browse multiple web pages in a Safari window using tabs.

Preview a tab

Simply hover the cursor over the tab.

Open a new tab

→ In the Safari application, click on the Add Tab icon ╬ on the toolbar.

Open the web page or PDF in a new tab

Carry out any of the below in the Safari application:

→ Cmd-click on a link on the web page.

→ Cmd-click on the Forward icon ⟩ or the Back icon ⟨ to go to the next or previous web page in another tab.

→ Write in the Search box, and then Command-click on one of the items in the search recommendations.

Open a tab in another window

In the Safari application, click Window> Move Tab to a New Window.

Reopen a recently closed tab

→ In the Safari application, click History> Recently Closed, and then select the website you'd like to reopen.

Hide advertisements when reading articles

Use Reader's View, to view a site article on a single page, designed for easy reading and without advertisements, navigations, or other distractions. You can change the font, background colour, & font size for Reader's view.

View articles in Reader's view

➔ In the Safari application, click on the Reader icon in the Search bar.

The icon will only appear if the website has content that Reader's view can show.

➜ To stop making use of Reader's View, click on the Reader button once more or press the Esc key on the keyboard.

Change how a webpage looks in Reader

➜ In the Safari application, while viewing an article in Reader's view, click on the Format icon AA in the search box.

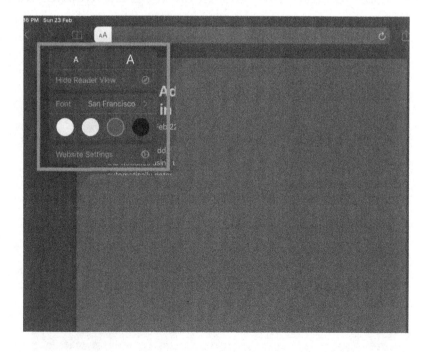

➜ Carry out any of the below to change the settings:

- Pick one of the font sizes.
- Pick a background colour.
- Select a font.

Translate a webpage

If you come across a site that's in a language you don't understand, you can use Safari to translate the text.

➜ Visit the website you want to translate
If the web page is translatable, you'll see the Translate icon in the search box.

➜ Click the Translation icon , and then choose one of the languages.

View items you've downloaded

➜ Click the Downloads icon close to the upper right edge of the Safari window.
The icon won't appear if the download list is empty.
➜ Carry out any of the below:

- Click on the Stop icon close to the filename in the download list to pause what you're downloading. Click the Continue icon ⟳ to resume.

- Look for a downloaded item on your iMac: Click on the Magnifier button 🔍 close to the filename in the download list.
- Clear the download list: Click on the **Clear** button in the download list. To remove an item, Ctrl-click on the item, then click on the **Remove From List** button.

Save a picture from a website

➜ Ctrl-click on the picture in the site
➜ Click on the Add Image to Photos, Save Image As, or the Save Image to Downloads button.

Interact with text in an image in the Safari browser

You can highlight the text in a picture, and then interact with the text, for instance, if an image shows an address, or e-mail address, you can use the text to get more info about the location in the Maps application or compose an e-mail.

→ In the Safari application, navigate to the picture that has text in it.
→ Hover the cursor over the text, and then drag to highlight the text.
→ Ctrl-click on the highlighted text.
→ Carry out any of the below:
- Copy text: Click on the **Copy** button and then paste it in a note, document, etc.
- Check the meaning of a word: Click on the Lookup button.
- Translate text: Click on Translate [text], and then pick one of the languages.
- Share the text: Click on the **Share** button, and then select one of the sharing options.
- Search for the text on the Internet: Click on Search with [web searching engine].
- Go to a site: Open the link in a browser.
- Contact a phone number: Choose to call the phone number, start a Face-Time call, or send a message to the phone number.
- See a map: Launch the Maps application to see a map of the address.
- Contact an e-mail address: Choose to write an e-mail or add the e-mail address to your Contacts list.

Change your homepage

The homepage is the webpage that appears when you open a new tab or window.

→ In the Safari application, click on Safari> Settings, and then click on General.
→ Type the website address in the box next to Homepage. To use the webpage you are currently viewing, click on the Set to Current Page button.

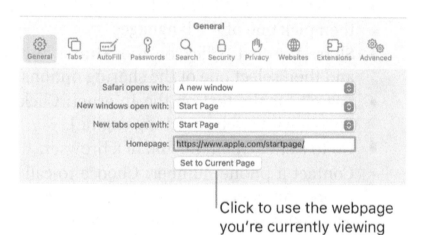

Click to use the webpage you're currently viewing as your homepage.

→ Select when your home page appears.
   • Open a new window with your home page: Click on the **New Window open with** drop-down menu, and then click on Homepage.

- Open a new tab with your home page: Click on the **New tab open with** drop-down menu, then click on Home page.

Customize the start page

You can put what is most important to you on the web in one place, the start page.

➔ In the Safari application, select Bookmarks> Show Starts Page

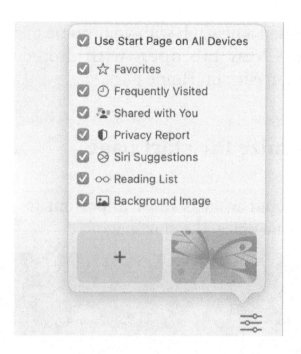

→ Click on the Options icon ⚏ in the lower right edge of the window.

→ Choose an option for your start page.

- Use Start Page on All Devices: Click on this option to use the same start page settings on all Apple devices that are using your Apple ID & have Safari activated in iCloud settings.

- iCloud Tabs: See pages that are open on your other Apple devices.

- Recently closed tabs.

- Tab Group Favorites.

- Siri Tips.

- Frequently Visited.

- Favourites
- Reading list: Show the websites you have chosen to read later.
- Privacy Report.
- Shared with you: See videos & other links that were shared with you via the Messages application.
- Background Image.

→ Drag start page options to arrange them the way you like

→ Click on the Safari window.

Allow or block pop-ups on a site

Pop-ups can be useful or annoying. Some sites require you to permit pop-ups. For instance, a bank's site may display your monthly statement in a pop-up. Other sites may fill your display with pop-up advertisements.

Adhere to the directives below to allow or block pops-up:

→ Visit the website in the Safari application.

→ Click on Safari> Settings, and then click on Websites.

Click Websites.

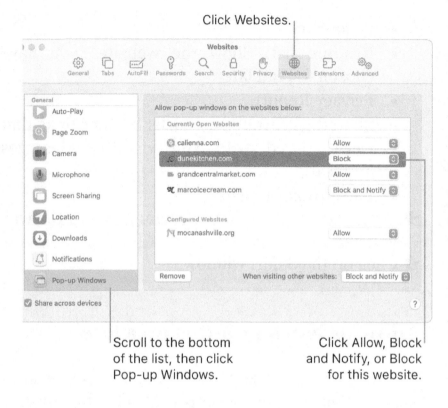

Scroll to the bottom of the list, then click Pop-up Windows.

Click Allow, Block and Notify, or Block for this website.

→ Click on Pop-ups Windows on the left side of the window. (You may have to scroll down)
→ In the drop-down menu for the site, pick any of the below:
- Blocked: Pop-ups will not appear on the site.
- Block & Notify: Pop-ups won't appear on the site, but when you visit a site, you can display the pops-up by clicking the Show icon in the Search field.

Click to show the blocked
pop-up windows.

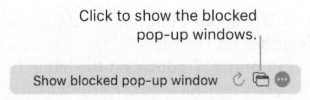

- Allow: Pop-ups will appear on the site.

Allow or block pop-ups on all sites

Click Remove to clear selections
from Configured Websites and
choose another setting.

Click Websites.

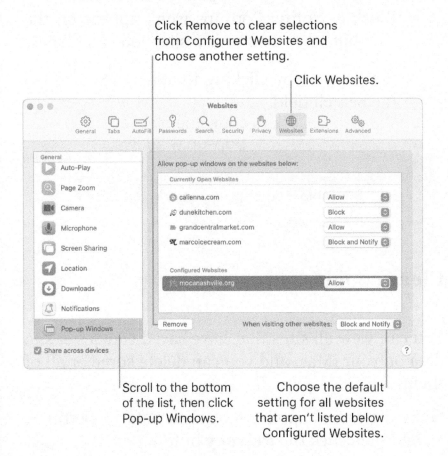

Scroll to the bottom
of the list, then click
Pop-up Windows.

Choose the default
setting for all websites
that aren't listed below
Configured Websites.

→ In the Safari application, click Safari> Settings, and then click on Websites.

→ Click on Pop-ups Windows on the left side of the window. (You may have to scroll down)

→ Click on the **When Visiting Other Websites** drop-down menu, and then pick any of the below:

- Blocked: Pop-ups will not appear on the sites.
- Allow: Pop-ups will appear on the sites.
- Block & Notify: Pop-ups won't appear on the site, but when you visit a site, you can display the pops-up by clicking the Show icon in the Search field.

Click to show the blocked
pop-up windows.

Show blocked pop-up window ↻ 🗖 ⚫

Clear cookies

You can view all sites that have saved cookies & site data on your iMac, and you can delete some or all of them.

→ In the Safari application, click Safari> Settings, and then click the **Privacy** button.

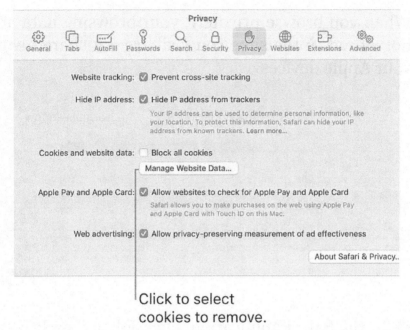

Click to select
cookies to remove.

➔ Click on the **Manage Websites data** button.
➔ Choose the sites, and then click on the Remove or Remove All button.

Clear your browsing history

➔ In the Safari application, click History> Clear History, and then click on the drop-down menu.
➔ Select how much data you want to clear.

Use Private browsing

When you browse privately, your browsing data are not stored, & the sites you visit are not shared with your Apple devices.

Private browsing window   Normal window

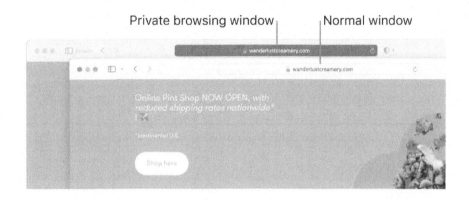

→ In the Safari application, click File> New Private Window, or go to a private window that has already been opened.
The search box of a private window is usually dark
→ Visit sites as you normally would

To leave Private browsing, simply close the window, and switch to a normal window or click File> New Windows to open a non-private window

CHAPTER 8

MAIL

Use the Mail application to manage all your e-mail accounts.

Add an email account in Mail

Adhere to the instructions below to add your existing e-mail accounts to the Mail application.

Choose a Mail account provider...

- ◉ iCloud
- ○ Microsoft Exchange
- ○ Google
- ○ yahoo!
- ○ Aol.
- ○ Other Mail Account...

?   Cancel   Continue

→ When you launch the Mail application for the first time, you'll be prompted to add an account. Pick one of the account types (like, yahoo, iCloud, Google for Gmail, etc.) or the **Other Mail Account** option, then fill in your account details

→ If you've added an e-mail account, you can add more. In the Mail application, click Mail, click on the **Add Accounts** button in the menu, select one of the account types, and then fill in your account details. Ensure you select the checkbox for the account type.

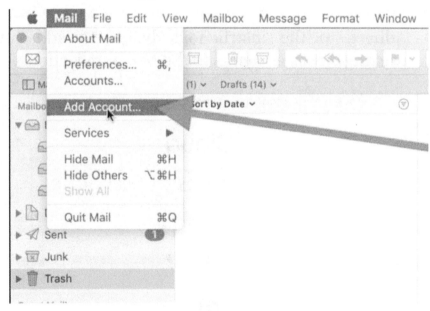

Log out of or temporarily disable e-mail accounts

You can temporarily stop making use of an e-mail account and then activate the account again when you need it. When you deactivate an account, its messages will stop appearing in the Mail app.

→ In the Mail application, click on Mail, and then click on the **Accounts** button in the menu.
→ Select the account you plan on deactivating, and then unselect the Mail's checkbox.

Simply select the Mail checkbox of the account when you want to start making use of it.

Remove email accounts from Mail

When you remove an e-mail account, the account's messages will be erased from your iMac

→ In the Mail application, click on Mail, click on the Settings button in the menu, and then click on Accounts.
→ Choose one of the accounts, and then click on the Remove icon — .

Note: If other applications are also using the account, you'll be prompted to remove the account in Internet Account settings. Click on the button to access Internet Account, and then deactivate Mail for the account. To stop making use of the account in all applications, ensure you select the account, and then click on the Remove icon — .

Compose & send an e-mail

→ Click the Compose Email icon ⬜ in the Mail tool bar.
→ In the address field (like Cc or To) of the message, type the name or e-mail address of the persons you want to send the message to.
  While typing, the Mail app will show email addresses that you've used before in Mail or that it found in the Contacts application
  Click on an address bar, and then click on the

  Add icon ⊕ that pops-up. Click on one of the contacts in the list, then click on the e-mail address (if available)
  To use another field, like Priority or Bcc, click on

  the Header button ⬚ ⌄ , then click a field.
→ If you have more than one email address registered in the Mail application, you can select the address you want to send the email from. To do this, simply hover the cursor over the From field in the e-mail, click on the drop-down menu that pops-up, and then pick any of the e-mail addresses

→ Type the subject of the e-mail and then add your message.
You can carry out any of the below:

- Click the Formatting icon Aa to change the styles, fonts, and more.

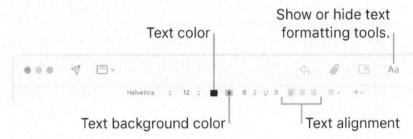

- Click on the Emoji icon ☺ to insert symbols & emoji.
- Select text and then translate it.
- Click the Add Attachments icon✐ or the Photos icon 🖼⌄ to add pictures or documents.

→ When you're done, click the Send icon ◁ .

Schedule an email with Send Later

Click on the drop-down menu close to the Send icon ◁ in an e-mail, and then select any of the options.

You can find the email in the Send Later mailbox in the side bar.

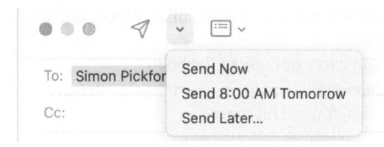

To: Simon Pickfor...

Cc:

Send Now

Send 8:00 AM Tomorrow

Send Later...

To change the scheduled time for the e-mail, simply double-click the e-mail in the Send Later mailbox, and then click on the **Edit** button in the upper right edge.

To prevent the e-mail from sending, simply select the e-mail, and then click on the Trash icon 🗑.

Unsend an email

Click to search for
an item in Mail.

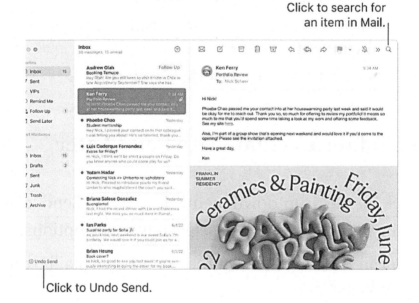

Click to Undo Send.

If you made a mistake in your e-mail or sent the wrong email, you can use the **Undo Send** feature to recall the e-mail. You are also allowed to set a delay for e-mails to give yourself enough time to unsend them.

→ In the Mail application, click on the **Undo Send** button at the lower part of the side bar within ten seconds of sending an e-mail.

Click to Undo Send.

Note: To change how long you have to unsend an e-mail or to deactivate the **Undo Send** feature, click on Mail, click on the **Settings** button in the menu, click on Composing, click on the "Undo send delay" drop-down menu, and then pick one of the options.

Reply or forward an email

1. In Mail, pick one of the messages from the messages list.

2. Hover the cursor over the message header, and then click any of the buttons below:

- The Reply button ↩ to reply to the sender only.
- The Reply All button ↩ to reply to the sender & others.
- The Forward button ↪ to select new recipients.

3. Type your response.
4. Click on the Send Email icon ✒ when you are done.

Use Remind Me to come back to emails later

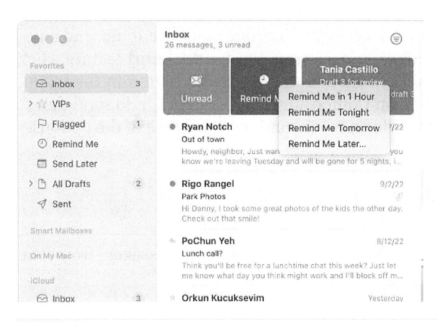

If you do not have time to respond to an e-mail at the moment, you can set a date & time to receive a reminder & push the message back to the top of your inbox.

➜ In Mail, select one of the messages, use 2 fingers to swipe right on the trackpad, and then click on the **Remind Me** button. Or just Ctrl-click the message.

➜ Choose any of the available options.
    If you picked the **Remind Me Later** option, simply set when you'd like to receive a reminder.

Delete emails

1. Select one or more messages in the Mail application.

2. Click on the Trash button 🗑 in the mail tool bar.

Search for emails

➜ In the Mail application, in the toolbar, type a phrase that can be found in the e-mail in the search box (if it does not appear, click on the Search icon 🔍 in the toolbar).

Save your search as a Smart Mailbox.

Type or paste text. Or drag an email address from a message.

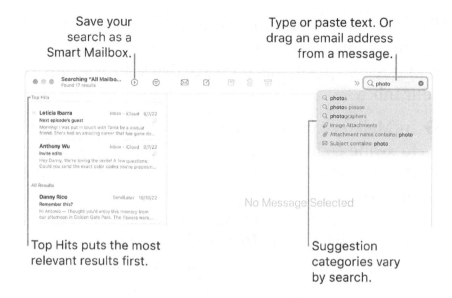

Top Hits puts the most relevant results first.

Suggestion categories vary by search.

→ Press the Return button on the keyboard and pick one of the results

→ When you are done, click on the Clear icon 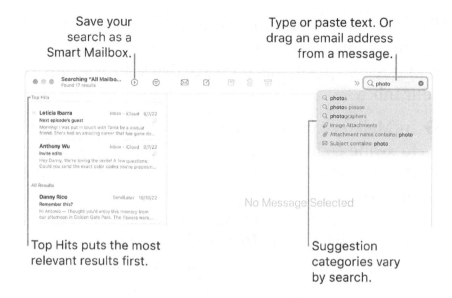 in the search box.

Use Mail Privacy Protection

The Mail application can protect your privacy. The e-mail messages you receive may contain extended content that allows the sender to collect info when you view the message, such as when and how often you view it, your IP address, and other information. The Mail Privacy Protection setting stops the sender from getting any information from you.

➜ In the Mail application, click on Mail, click on the **Settings** button in the menu, and then click on Privacy.

➜ Select **Protect mail activity**.

When you select this option, your IP address will be hidden from email senders, and remote contents are privately downloaded in the background when you receive a message not when you view it.

CHAPTER 9

APPLE PAY

You can use Apple Pay to make safe & private purchases on your Mac.

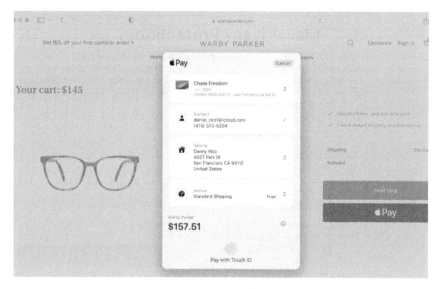

Change wallet and Apple Pay settings

→ Click on the Apple menu icon in the upper left part of your display, click on the **Systems Setting** button in the menu, and then click on the **Wallet and Apple Pay** button in the side bar

➔ Carry out any of the below:

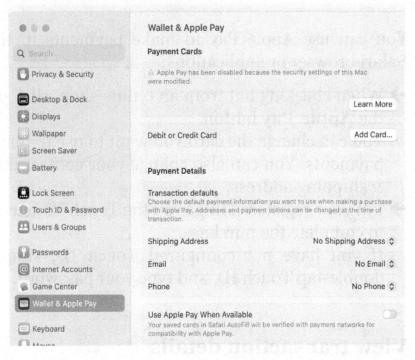

> ➤ Add card: You can use your iMac's camera to scan your card or type the card details. Click on the **Add Card** button, and then adhere to the directives on the screen.
> ➤ Default card: Select one of your cards to use it as your primary card for payment.
> ➤ Shipping Address
> ➤ Email
> ➤ Phone
> ➤ Apple Pay & privacy

To remove a card from Apple Pay, click on the card, and then click on the **Remove Card** button.

Make payments with Apple Pay

You can use Apple Pay to make payments in the Safari browser or applications.

→ When checking out from an online shop, click on the **Apple Pay** button.
  You can change the card you want to use to make payments. You can also change your contact info & shipping address.
→ Put your registered finger on the Touch ID sensor to complete the purchase.
  If you have not configured Touch ID, simply double-tap Touch ID, and type your password.

View transaction details

→ Click on the Apple menu icon in the upper left part of your display, click on the **System Settings** button in the menu, and then click on the **Wallet and Apple Pay** button in the side bar

→ Click on a card, and then activate the "Show Transaction Notifications" feature.

The last transactions related to the selected card will be displayed on the right.

CHAPTER 10

FACETIME

Use the FaceTime application to make voice & video calls from your iMac to other people.

FaceTime requirements

You have to meet the following requirements before you can make video & voice calls with FaceTime:

→ Connect to the Internet
→ Sign in to FaceTime using your Apple ID

Log in to FaceTime on your device

The first time you enter the Face-Time application, you will be prompted to log in.

→ Fill in your Apple ID details in the FaceTime application.
→ Click on "Next" to sign in. FaceTime would be activated automatically.

Sign out of or turn off FaceTime

In the FaceTime application, carry out any of the below:

→ Log out of Face-Time: Click on FaceTime, click on the **Settings** button in the menu, click on General, and then click on Sign Out.

→ Deactivate FaceTime: Click on FaceTime, and click on **Turn Off FaceTime** in the menu. To reactivate FaceTime, simply click on the **Turn On** button.

Make a FaceTime call

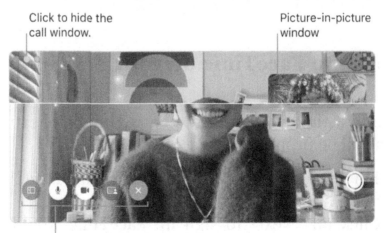

Click to hide the call window.

Picture-in-picture window

Move the pointer over FaceTime to see call options.

➔ Enter the FaceTime application, and click on the **New FaceTime** button.
➔ Carry out any of the below to add callers to the New FaceTime window:

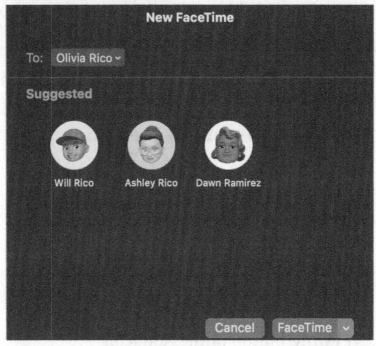

- Type the number or e-mail address of the individual you plan on calling. You may have to press the Return key on the keyboard.
- If the individual is on your contacts list, you can simply type the name of the individual or choose from the Suggested list.

➔ To make a group call, simply repeat the steps above till you add all the participants.

→ Click on the **FaceTime** button to make a video call. To make a voice call, click on the down arrow ∨ and then click on Face-Time Audio.

To send an audible notification to callers who have not yet joined the call, click the Sidebar icon⌷▢, & then click on the **Ring** button.

Add more people to the call

While on a Face-Time call, you can add more individuals to the call, even if you're not the one who started the call.

→ While on a FaceTime call, simply click on the Sidebar icon⌷▢, and then click on the **Add People** button or the Add icon⊕.

→ Carry out any of the below:
- Type the number or email address of the individual you plan on calling. You may have to press the Return key on the keyboard.
- If the person is on your contacts list, you can simply type the name of the person or choose from the Suggested list.
  To add multiple individuals at the same time, simply fill in each person's contact info in the To field.

→ Click on the **Add** button

End a call

Adhere to the directives below to end a call in the FaceTime application on your iMac:

→ End a voice call: Click on the End call icon .
→ End a video call: Hover the cursor over the window, and then click on the End button .

Accept a Face-Time call

→ When an alert pops-up in the upper-right corner of your iMac's display, carry out any of the below:
  ➢ Accept a call: Click on the **Accept** button.
  ➢ Accept a video call as a voice call: Click on the Down Arrow ∨ beside Accept, and then select the **Answer as Audio** option.
  ➢ Accept a call & end the current call: Click on the **End and Accept** button.
  ➢ Accept a call & put the current call on Hold: Click on the **Hold and Accept** button.
  ➢ Join a Face-Time Group call: Click on the **Join** button, and then click on the Join Call icon in the FaceTime application window.

Reject Face-Time calls

Send a text message or create a reminder.

→ When an alert pops-up in the upper-right corner of your iMac's display, carry out any of the below:
   ➢ Click on the **Decline** button to reject a call.
   ➢ Decline a call & send a message or set a reminder to call back later: Click on the Down Arrow ∨ close to Decline, click on one of the options, and adhere to the guidelines on your display.

Create & share a link to a Face-Time call

You can create a Face-Time call link & share it with others.

→ Launch the Face-Time application on your iMac, and carry out any of the below:

- Create a link to a new call: Click on the **Create Link** button.
- Create a link to the current call: Click on the Sidebar icon ⊡ , and then click on the **Create Link** button.
- Share a link to a previous call: Click on the Information icon ⓘ , and then click on the Share icon ⬆ .

➜ Select any of the sharing options.

To join a call from a FaceTime link, simply click or touch the link, and then adhere to the instructions on your display to start or join the call.

Allow callers to join Face-Time calls

A badge will appear on the Sidebar icon ⊡ when someone is requesting to join the call.

➜ While on a Face-Time call, click on the Sidebar icon when you see a badge on the icon ⊡ .

➜ Carry out any of the below:

   ➤ Click on the Approve icon ✓ to let the caller in.

   ➤ Click on the Decline button ✕ if you don't want the caller to join the call

To mute the audio alert when someone joins the FaceTime call, click on the Sidebar icon⬚, and then click on the **Silence Join Request** button.

Delete a FaceTime link

→ In the FaceTime application, check the calls list to see the call you made with a Face-Time link

→ Click on the Information iconⓘ, and then click on the **Delete Link** button

Use SharePlay to share your screen in Face-Time

The SharePlay feature allows you to share what's on your screen with other people in the video call. You can show applications, websites, & more during a Face-Time video call.

→ While making a FaceTime call, launch the application you'd like to share in the FaceTime video call.

→ Click on the FaceTime Video icon▢ in the menu bar.

→ Click on the Share Display icon 🖼, and then carry out any of the below:

➢ Share an application window: Click on Window, hover the cursor to the window you plan on sharing, and then click on the **Share This Window** button.

➢ Share all windows from an application: Click on App, hover the cursor to the window you'd like to share, and then click on the **Share All[Application] Window** button

➢ Share multiple windows: While Sharing 1 or more windows, click on the **Add Window** button. To stop sharing a window, simply click on the Minus icon ➖ in the window's preview.

➢ Share the entire screen: Click Screen, hover the cursor to anywhere on your display, and then click on the **Share Screen** button.

➢ Change the window you are sharing: Hold the cursor over the shared window preview, click on the **Change Shared Window** button, hover the cursor to the window you'd like to share, and then click on the **Share This Window** button.

To stop sharing, click on the Display Sharing button ⬤ in the menu bar, and then click on **Stop Sharing**.

Use Presenter Overlay during video conferencing

You can use the Presenter Overlay feature in a FaceTime video call so that others in the call can see you and the screen you are sharing at the same time. The big overlay places your shared screen beside you while you stay prominent so that you can move & talk in front of the screen. The small overlay puts your face in a bubble that can be moved around, so it's easy to see you while you showcase your work.

→ To use Presenter Overlay, click on the Video button in the menu bar.

➜ Pick one of the Presenter Overlay sizes. When you share the screen, the overlay will appear immediately.

To deactivate Presenter Overlay, click the Video button 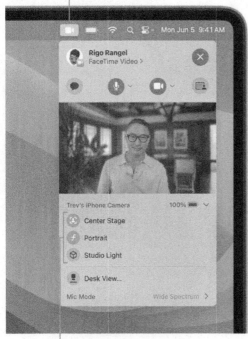 in the menu bar, click Off under Presenter Overlay

Use video effects in FaceTime calls

Appears when you're in a FaceTime call.

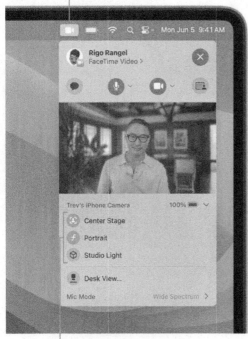

Lists available video effects for the selected camera.

Use video effects to place the focus on you or your reactions while making FaceTime video calls.

Use hand gestures to add reactions

You can use hand gestures to add reactions—visual effects that you use to express how you're feeling during a video call.

Choose one of the reactions below:

Reactions	Gestures	Icons
Fireworks		
Lasers		
Confetti		
Rain		
Balloons		

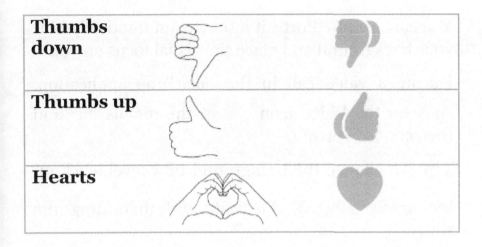

Thumbs down		
Thumbs up		
Hearts		

Note: When making use of hand gestures, hold your hands away from your face, and pause for a few seconds to activate the reaction effects.

To add reactions without using hand gestures, click on the Video icon 📹 in the menu bar, click the arrow ⟩ beside Reactions, and then click on one of the options. (If you cannot find the arrow, click on the **Reactions** button to activate the feature.)

To disable the Reactions feature, click the Video icon 📹 in the menus bar and click the **Reactions** button.

Blur your background

You can activate Portrait mode to automatically blur your background and place the visual focus on you.

During a video call in the FaceTime application, click on the Video icon ▣ in the menus bar and then choose Portrait.

Tip: To change the background blur level, click on the arrow ❯ beside Portrait, and then drag the slider.

To deactivate Portrait mode, click on the Video icon ▣ in the menus bar, and then unselect Portrait.

Activate or deactivate Center Stage

Centre Stage keeps you and anybody close to you, centered in the frame as you move around while in the FaceTime video call.

During a video call in the FaceTime application, click on the Video icon ▣ in the menus bar and then choose Centre Stage.

To deactivate Centre Stage, click on the Video icon ▣ in the menus bar, and then unselect Center Stage.

Use Studio Light

You can use Studio Light to darken the background and brighten your face.

During a video call in the FaceTime application, click on the Video icon  in the menus bar and then choose Studio Light.

Tip: To change the Studio Light level, click on the arrow ❯ beside Studio Light, and then drag the slider.

To deactivate Studio Light, click on the Video icon ▣ in the menus bar, and then unselect Studio Light.

Capture Live Photos in a Face-Time call

Live Photo button

While on a FaceTime video call, you can capture Live Photos of a participant. You and the participant will be notified that a picture was taken, and the picture will be stored in the Photos library.

Configure FaceTime for Live Photos

→ In the Face-Time application, click on FaceTime, click on Settings in the menu, and then click on the **General** button
→ Tick the **Allow Live Photos to be captured in video calls** check box.

Setup the Photos application for Live Photos

Launch the Photos application on your iMac if you haven't already.

Capture Live Photos

→ Carry out any of the below while on a Face-Time video call:
  ➢ On a single call: Select the Face-Time window.
  ➢ On a group call: Double-click the participant's tile.
→ Click on the Capture button ◯ .

Live Photo button

You can find the Live Photo in the Photos application.

Change audio options for FaceTime calls

Appears when you're in a FaceTime call.

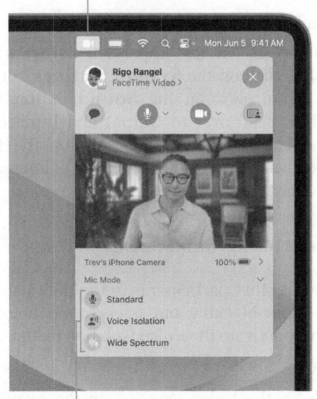

Depending on your Mac, you can change the audio effects.

Mute or change FaceTime call volume

Carry out any of the below while on a Face-Time call:

→ Mute your device: In the Face-Time application, hover the cursor over the call window, then click

on the Mute icon 🎤 .
Click on the icon one more time to unmute your iMac.

→ Change the Mic volume: Click on the Apple

menu icon 🍎 in the upper left corner of your display, click on the **System Settings** button in the menu, click on the **Sound** button in the sidebar, head over to Output and Input on the right side of your display, click on the **Input** button, and then slide the Input Volume slider. (You may have to scroll.)

Filter out background noise

If you want other participants in the call to hear you clearly while blocking out background noise, you can simply activate the Voice Isolation feature.

→ Activate Voice Isolation while on a video call:

Click on the Video icon 📹 in the menus bar, and then click on the down arrow ∨ close to the

Mic button 🎤. Click on the right arrow ❯ beside **Mic Mode**, and then click on the **Voice Isolation** button.

→ Activate the Voice Isolation feature in a voice call: In the FaceTime application, click on the Audio icon 🎤 in the menu bar, and then click on the **Voice Isolation** button.

Add background sounds

If you want other participants in the call to hear your voice & the noise around you, you can simply activate the Wide Spectrum feature.

→ Activate Wide Spectrum while on a video call: Click on the Video icon 🎥 in the menus bar, and then click on the down arrow ﹀ close to the Mic button 🎤. Click on the right arrow ❯ beside **Mic Mode**, and then click on the **Wide Spectrum** button.

→ Activate the Wide Spectrum feature in a voice call: In the FaceTime application, click on the Audio icon 🎤 in the menu bar, and then click on the **Wide Spectrum** button.

Activate Live Captions in Face-Time

You can activate the Live Captions feature to see the discussion transcribed on your display. If you have trouble hearing the conversation, the Live Captions feature can make it easy for you to follow.

➜ While on a Face-Time video call, select Live Captions in the side bar.
If you can't find the side bar, click on the Sidebar icon in the lower part of the window.
➜ If prompted, click the **Download** button.

Deselect Live Captions in the side bar to disable this feature

Change FaceTime ringtones

➜ In the Face-Time application, click on FaceTime, click on the **Settings** button in the menu, and then click on the **General** button
➜ Click on the Ringtone drop-down menu, and then click on one of the ringtones

Block callers on FaceTime

➜ In the FaceTime application, click on FaceTime, click on Settings in the menu, and then click on Blocked.

➜ Click on the Add icon ╋ , and then choose one of the names in the contacts list.
You can also block a caller from the recent calls list, by simply Ctrl-clicking the contact, and then clicking on the **Block This Caller** button.

To unblock a caller, click on FaceTime, click on Settings in the menu, and then click on the **Blocked** button. Select one of the names in the list, and then click on the Remove icon ━ .

Delete your FaceTime call history

Carry out any of the below in the FaceTime application:

➜ Delete a call: Ctrl-click on a call, and then click on the **Remove from Recents** button

➜ Delete all recent calls: Click on FaceTime, and then click on the **Remove All Recents** button in the menu.

CHAPTER 11

USE YOUR MAC WITH OTHER APPLE DEVICES

Unlock your iMac & approve requests with your Apple Watch

When you are wearing your Apple Watch and close to your iMac, you can use your smartwatch to unlock your iMac or approve application requests, without entering a passcode.

Note: To use these features, ensure your Apple Watch is on your wrist and close to your iMac. Also, make sure you are using the same Apple ID on your iMac and your watch, and 2-factor authentication is activated for your Apple ID.

Activate Auto Unlock and Approve with Apple Watch

➔ Click on the Apple menu icon in the upper left corner of your display, click on the **System Settings** button in the menu, and then click on Touch ID & Passcode in the sidebar

→ Head over to Apple Watch on the right side of the window, and then activate the option close to your watch's name.

Unlock your iMac

Move the mouse or press any key on the keyboard to wake your iMac from its idle state. The screen will indicate that your iMac has been unlocked.

Approve application requests

Whenever an application requires authentication on your iMac, for things like viewing passwords, unlocking settings or notes, & approving application installations, an approval request from your iMac will appear on your smartwatch.

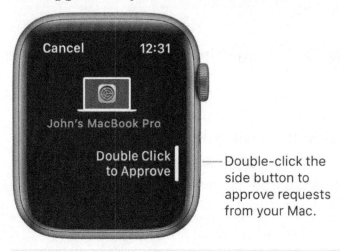

Double-click the side button to approve requests from your Mac.

Double-press your watch's side button to approve the request.

Use your iPhone as a webcam on your iMac

With the **Continuity Camera** feature, you can use your iPhone as your iMac's microphone or webcam, and take advantage of your iPhone's video effects.

Getting Started

Before using the Continuity Camera setting, you must:

→ Ensure your iMac is running macOS 13 or after and your iPhone is using iOS 16 or after.
→ Make sure you are using the same Apple ID on both devices, and 2-factor authentication is activated for your Apple ID.

→ Activate Bluetooth & WiFi on your iMac & iPhone
→ Mount your iPhone: Your iPhone must be near your iMac, Locked, Stable, & positioned with its back camera facing you without any obstruction

Use your iPhone as a microphone or webcam

→ Open any app on your iMac that can access the microphone or camera, such as Face-Time or Photos Booth.
→ In the application's menu bar or setting, pick your iPhone as the microphone or camera. (For example, in the FaceTime application, click on the **Video** button in the menu bar, and then choose your iPhone as the camera. Or, in Photos Booth, click on the **Camera** button in the menu bar, and then choose your iPhone as the camera.)

The Continuity application will open on your iPhone and start streaming video or audio from the back camera to your iMac.

➜ Carry out any of the below:

- Pause the audio or video: Touch the Pause button on your phone or unlock your iPhone.
- Resume the audio or video: Touch the **Resume** button on your phone, or lock your iPhone.
- Stop using your phone as a microphone or webcam: Quit the application on your iMac.
- Remove your phone as an option: Touch the **Disconnect** button on your iPhone, and confirm that you want to disconnect.
  To reconnect your iPhone, simply use a USB cable to connect your phone to your iMac.

Automatically switch to your iPhone's camera

Your iMac can automatically use your iPhone as its camera for some Mac applications, such as Photos Booth & FaceTime. To do this, your iPhone must:

➜ Be near your iMac
➜ Be in landscape orientation
➜ Be stationary
➜ Not be lying flat

→ Have its back camera facing you without any obstructions

→ Have its screen off.

If you have used your phone as a webcam on your iMac before, other applications on your iMac might also remember your iPhone as your preferred camera.

Make your iPhone the default microphone

You can turn your iPhone into the primary microphone for your iMac.

→ Click on the Apple menu icon in the upper left corner of your display, click on System Settings, and then click the **Sound** button on the sidebar.

→ Choose your phone from the sound input devices list.
The Continuity application will open on your iPhone & start capturing sound.

If your iPhone does not appear as a microphone or camera option

If your iPhone does not appear in the microphone or camera list in a Sound or application settings, try the following:

→ Use a USB cable to connect your phone to your iMac and check again. (If it is already connected by cable, disconnect and reconnect.)
→ Make sure of the following:
- You are using an iPhone XR or after.
- Your iPhone is using iOS 16.0 or after.
- Your iMac is using macOS 13.0 or after.
- Your iPhone has the Continuity Camera feature activated in the Settings application> General> AirPlay & Handoff.
- Your iPhone accepts your iMac as a trusted computer.
- Both your iPhone & iMac have Bluetooth, WiFi, and two-factor authentication activated.
- Your iMac & iPhone are using the same Apple ID
- Your iMac & iPhone are close to each other.
- Your iPhone is not sharing its mobile connection, and your iMac is not sharing its internet connection.
- Your chosen video application has been updated to the most recent version.

Continuity Camera

The Continuity Camera feature allows you can take a photo or scan a document with an iPad or iPhone and have the picture or scanned document instantly appear on your iMac, just where you need it—for instance, in a folder, note, e-mail, or document.

Before using the Continuity Camera setting, you must:

→ Ensure your iMac, iPad, & iPhone are using the latest version of macOS, iPadOS, & iOS.
→ Make sure you are using the same Apple ID on both devices, and 2-factor authentication is activated for your Apple ID.
→ Activate Bluetooth & WiFi on your iMac & iPhone

Adhere to the directives below to use the Continuity Camera feature:

➜ On your iMac, place the cursor where you want to insert the scanned document or picture.
For instance, in an e-mail, note, or document.

➜ Click on File, click on Insert from iPad or iPhone in the menu, and then click on Scan Documents or Take Photo.

In some applications, you can click on File, click on the **Import from iPad or iPhone** button in the menu, and click on Take Photos or Scan

Document to create a new file with scans or pictures. You can also Ctrl-click a folder or the desktop in a Finder window, click on Import from iPad or iPhone, and then click on Scan Document or Take Photos.

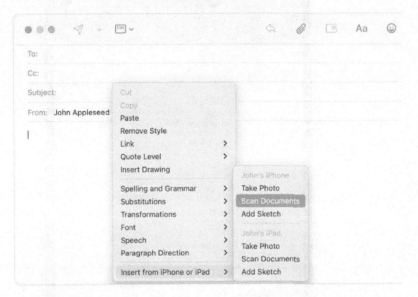

If the commands are not available in the File menu, they may be in a different menu (e.g. the Insert or Edit menu), or the application you are using may not support Continuity Camera.

→ Carry out any of the below on your iPad or iPhone:

- For a picture: Capture the picture, and then click on the **Use Photo or Retake** button.
- For a scan: Scan the document. Your iPhone will detect the edges of the document and automatically adjust the area covered— if you

want to manually adjust the edges, simply drag the frame. When you are done, touch the **Keep Scan** button or the **Retake** button.

→ On your iMac, then scanned document or photo will appear where you placed the cursor or, if you started from a folder or the desktop, as a file.

Handoff

The Handoff feature allows you to start something on one Apple device and pick it up on another Apple device seamlessly. For instance, you can start replying to an e-mail on your iPad, and finish the e-mail in the Mail application on your iMac. The Handoff feature is compatible with many Apple applications, like Safari, Pages, Contacts, etc. Some 3rd party applications might also work with the Handoff feature.

To use the **Handoff** feature, you must activate Handoff, Bluetooth, & WiFi on your iMac, iPad &

iPhone. You must also sign in with the same Apple ID on both Apple devices.

Enable or disable Handoff

→ On your iMac: Click on the Apple menu icon , click on the **System Settings** button, click on General in the sidebar, click on AirDrop & Handoff on the right side of the window, and then activate or disable "**Allow Handoff between this iMac & your iCloud devices**"

→ On iPad or iPhone: Head over to the Settings application, touch General, touch AirPlay & Handoff, and then activate or disable **Handoff**.

→ On your Apple Watch: Launch the Apple Watch application on your iPhone, touch the **My Watch** tab, touch General, and then activate or disable the **Enable Handoff** feature.

Hand off between devices

→ From your iMac to an iPad or iPhone: The Handoff icon of the application you are making use of on your iMac will appear at the bottom of the Apps Switcher on your iPhone or at the end of the Dock on your iPad. Touch the button to continue working in the application.

→ From an iPad, iPhone, or Apple Watch to your iMac: The Handoff icon of the application you are using on your Apple Watch, iPad, or iPhone will appear on your iMac close to the right end of the Dock. Click on the icon to continue working in the application.
You can also press Command-Tab to switch to the application that has the Handoff icon.

Universal Clipboard

The **Universal Clipboard** feature allows you to copy videos, pictures, & text on an Apple device and then paste them on another Apple device. For instance, you can copy a block of text from your iMac and paste it into a note in the Notes application on your nearby iPhone. Or copy files from a MacBook Air to paste into a folder on your iMac.

To use the **Universal Clipboard** feature, you must activate Handoff, Bluetooth, & WiFi on your iMac, iPad & iPhone. You must also sign in with the same Apple ID on both Apple devices.

Enable or disable Handoff

→ On your iMac: Click on the Apple menu icon, click on the **System Settings** button, click on General in the sidebar, click on AirDrop & Handoff on the right side of the window, and then activate or disable "**Allow Handoff between this iMac & your iCloud devices**"

→ On iPad or iPhone: Head over to the Settings application, touch General, touch AirPlay & Handoff, and then activate or disable **Handoff**.

→ On your Apple Watch: Launch the Apple Watch application on your iPhone, touch the **My Watch** tab, touch General, and then activate or disable the **Enable Handoff** feature.

Adhere to the directives below to use the Universal Clipboard feature:

→ Copy on a device: Select the content you'd like to copy, and then copy it. For instance, on your iMac, press the Command-C keyboard combination or click on Edit, and then click on the **Copy** button in the menu.
The copied content will be available to paste for a short time.

→ Paste on a device: Place the cursor where you want to paste the content, and then paste the content.

INDEX

V

volume, 76, 77, 78, 220
Volume, 25, 220

W

wallpaper, 36, 58, 104,
106, 108, 116

webcam, 226, 227, 228,
229
widgets, 45, 50
WiFi, 9, 37, 51, 70, 227,
230, 231, 235, 237

Made in the USA
Las Vegas, NV
27 February 2024